Bulbs

Marco Leone

Bulbs

Introduction by Rossella Rossi

FIREFLY BOOKS

In collaboration with

A FIREFLY BOOK

The foundation known as the International Flower Bulb Centre (IFBC), based in Hillegom, Holland, provides Dutch flower bulb growers and traders with international promotion for their bulbs and flowers. These collective promotional activities were initiated when growers and traders, working co-operatively, founded the Central Flower Bulb Committee in 1925. Today, the IFBC is active in Europe, North America and Asia and promotes flower bulb cultivation and awareness around the globe.

We would like to thank the IFBC for having provided the photographic material for this book.

Art Director
Giorgio Seppi

Editor
Tatjana Pauli

Cover design
Elena Dal Maso

Typesetting
Studio Grafico Clara Bolduri, Milan

Illustrations
Vittorio Salarolo

Translated by Andrée Mey

Published in Canada in 2003 by
Firefly Books Ltd.
3680 Victoria Park Avenue
Willowdale, Ontario M2H 3K1

Published in the U.S. in 2003 by
Firefly Books (U.S.) Inc.
P.O. Box 1338
Ellicott Station
Buffalo, New York 14205

Published by Firefly Books Ltd.
2003

First printing 2002

Publisher Cataloging-in-Publication Data (U.S.)
Leone, Marco.
 Bulbs : a Firefly guide / Marco Leone. 1st ed.
[256] p. : col. ill. , photos. ; cm.
Includes bibliographical references and index.
Summary: A comprehensive guide to 240 flowering bulbs including photographs, dimensions, origins and cultivation tips.
ISBN 1-55297-704-8 (pbk.)
1. Bulbs. I. Title.
631.526 21   SB425.L46 2003

National Library of Canada Cataloguing in Publication Data
Leone, Marco
 Bulbs: a Firefly guide / Marco Leone ; translated by Andrée Thibert Mey.
Translation of Bulbi.
Includes bibliographical references and index.
ISBN 1-55297-704-8
1. Bulbs. I. Mey, Andrée Thibert II. Title.
SB425.L46 2003   635.9'4
C2002-903837-5

Printed in Spain
D.L.TO: 1232/2002

CONTENTS

Key to symbols

Type of bulb

Bulb

Tuber

Corm

Rhizome

Tuberous root

Good cut flower

Good for forcing and growing
in containers

Fragrant flower

This book brings practical gardening information, scientific rigor and common sense advice together in an easy-to-use format.

The bulbs described in this survey are divided into two main sections: spring bulbs (bulbs that bloom in the spring) and summer bulbs (bulbs that bloom in the summer), but these categories are not overly rigid. In fact, the first spring bulbs actually bloom in late winter and many of the last summer bulbs actually bloom in the fall.

The scientific names (e.g., *Cyclamen coum*) have been given for each species, but the common names are generally used throughout the text (e.g., calla lilies, rather than *Zantedeschia*).

Each section is organized alphabetically by species or cultivar name, if it is a cultivated variety (e.g., Lilium Casa Blanca). While Casa Blanca may not have the same noble ring to it as *candidus*, these commercial names are important to know when ordering from bulb catalogs or finding your way around the local garden center.

For each of the approximately 300 varieties of flowering bulbs described in this survey, all of the essential information has been provided, including soil requirements, sun exposure, fertilizers, irrigation, storage techniques, propagation, average height and color. Other interesting and useful information, such as whether it makes a good cut flower, if it can be forced and if it has a fragrance, has also been provided. While the most space has naturally been granted to the most common bulbs, many of the lesser-known bulbs are also fully described.

Finally, in the larger genera, where species share many of the same characteristics (e.g., *Tulipa* and *Narcissi*), the same information is not repeated, but a different piece of information is given under each species heading. Therefore, by reviewing the whole genus, the reader will find all of the necessary information, but without having to see it repeated for each description.

INTRODUCTION

A modern hyacinth flower farm. Dutch floriculturists are the largest producers of bulbs and bulbous plants in Europe.

FLOWERING BULBS

Plants have solved the problem of survival during harsh seasons (cold winters, or overly hot and dry summers) in many different ways. Annuals generally turn to seed at the end of each season and these seeds are then able to stay alive for periods that can range from a few days to several years or, in some rare cases, even decades or centuries.

Other kinds of plants, however, rely on special underground storage organs, generically known as "bulbs." This unique ability to store nutrients makes bulbs easier to cultivate because they are hardier than other plants (at least during the initial phases of development) and able to tolerate very diverse climatic conditions. Bulbs are also easy to transplant or store for long periods of time because they are dormant for many months of the year. They can even be planted indoors and forced to bloom during the winter if handled properly. Beginning with the naturally occurring species of bulbous plants, floriculturists, over the past few centuries, have cultivated countless new varieties and hybrids. Although generally referred to as "bulbs," the category also includes tubers, corms, rhizomes and tuberous roots.

HISTORY AND TRADITIONS

Many bulbs are inextricably linked to important historical periods. Cassavas, sweet potatoes and yams, for example, were staple foods for many primitive societies. Onions and leeks were highly prized by the Egyptians, and potatoes were of vital importance to the *indios* of South America. Also, saffron—extracted from the pistils of *Crocus sativus*—was for centuries at the center of Minoan trade and commerce. The Minoans exported the saffron all over the known world, where it was not only used as a spice, but also as a dye, a perfume and a very potent medicine. Saffron is still today a highly valued and very costly product.

Other species of bulbous plants, on the other hand, were more valued for the aesthetic beauty of their flowers. The iris—most likely *Iris pseudacorus*—was the symbol of the kings of France for many centuries. The lily (*Lilium candidum*), already well known in ancient Crete and in the times of King Solomon of Israel, was of ritualistic value to the Greeks who associated the flower with Hera, the goddess of women, marriage and childbirth. According to Greek myth, Aphrodite, the goddess of love and fertility, mischievously gave the flower its phallic pistil. In Christian iconography, however, the lily symbolizes purity and in fact it often appears in the hand of the angel Gabriel *without* the pistil.

But the most extraordinary events in bulb history involve the tulip. Although never mentioned by the great classical authors, such as Dioscorides, Theophrastus and Pliny—to whom the flower was evidently not known—it does appear in the writings of the Persian poets of the 13th and 14th centuries. During the 1500s, the tulip was a recurring ornamental motif.

Lilies, gladioli and tulips monopolize the bulb world, but there is still plenty of room for crocuses (above) and daffodils (left).

This 16th century Turkish miniature illustrates a ceremony in the court of Murab III in which a giant artificial tulip is displayed to his astonished guests.

However, Flemish diplomat, Ogier Ghislain de Busbecq, ambassador to Ferdinand I of Austria, in the court of Suleiman the Magnificent in Constantinople, was the first European to learn of the tulip's existence. In 1554, on the road from Adrianopolis to Constantinople, the ambassador was struck by this beautiful flower that bloomed during the winter. He soon began to notice that the Turks were willing to pay large sums for the most rare and beautiful varieties, and shortly after tulips made their triumphant debut in the imperial gardens in Vienna. However, the tulip did not become available for mass consumption until some years later, when the Flemish botanist Carolus Clusius left Austria for the city of Leiden in the Netherlands, bringing with him some bulbs of the precious flower. Upon arrival, Clusius planted the bulbs in his own garden, and for some time was able to dissuade those who expressed interest in purchasing this new and exotic flower by asking exorbitant sums of money. This continued until one night someone furtively slipped into his garden and extracted the flowers and bulbs. These bulbs were reproduced in large quantities, which marked the beginning of a thriving industry. Shortly thereafter it was discovered that in propagating the bulbs, new colors would appear in the next generation they could breed; these apparently had nothing in common with their progenitors. It was not until the 19th century that it was proven that this phenomenon is actually caused by a virus.

This newfound breeding technique created a tulip craze, as the consumer was attracted to the idea that, in theory, these hybrid bulbs contained a new surprise. From 1634 to 1637 prices soared, while the so-called "tulipomania" spread to the entire population—nobles and peasants alike. But the market soon became saturated and prices crashed abruptly. The end of tulipomania was epitomized by Evrard Forstius, Professor of Botany at the University of Leiden, who was in the habit of destroying any tulips that happened to cross his path with his cane. However, considering that the Netherlands still grows and sells billions of tulip bulbs per year, perhaps tulipomania never really ended.

Tulipomania has long since passed, but a healthy passion for all varieties of tulips still exists, from the classic monotone tulip to the more imaginative and innovative modern varieties (at left, and at bottom of opposite page).

BEAUTIFUL ANYWHERE

Whoever loves flowers and has a little plot of land will find great allies in bulbous plants, and the numerous species and varieties available today can satisfy almost any demand. There are varieties that bloom in autumn, or even in winter; varieties best suited for sun or for shade, for damp or for dry soil, or for rock gardens; there are even climbing varieties. Any patch of earth, if planned with patience and the spirit of observation, can be transformed into a garden that is always in bloom—and you don't necessarily have to be a professional to obtain excellent results! However, some basic information about the area to be planted should be compiled before you begin, such as history of the site, type of terrain, average temperature, highs and lows at different times of the year, sun exposure, prevailing winds, etc. Once this information has been collected, the only thing left to do is to dream up your garden, and to choose plants that are best suited for making it a reality—this is the most difficult part, but don't get discouraged!

Every plant has special needs and these needs must be kept in mind at all times. The following tables and species identifications are, in this sense, a useful reference. However, none of these tools can take the place of experience, so keep a detailed diary of your experiences as you go; you will find it will become one of your most useful references.

Flowerbeds and borders

Almost all of the species listed in the following chapters are well suited to planting in flowerbeds and borders, naturally keeping in mind climate, size (the smallest species generally need to be placed towards the front), color, etc. Plants that are particularly decorative should be slightly elevated, like the giant lilies (*Cardiocrinum giganteum*) and *Eremurus robustus*.

• **Plants with the ability to naturalize.** A species is naturalized when it reproduces and spreads spontaneously, with no human intervention. In order for this to occur, the ecological needs of the plant must be fully met. It is usually necessary to plant hardy species

Many bulbs grow well both in the garden and in containers, as shown in the splendid multicolored species on the opposite page. Above and left, daffodils and fritillaries.

A garden is a constantly changing canvas of colors where delicate brushstrokes of harmony and discord are used to create its many masterpieces.

that grow in the wild in similar environments and to plant a good number of bulbs. This practice, most suitable for lawns and large gardens, is well worth the effort, because it reduces care to a minimum and creates spectacular blooming seasons. *Allium, Anemone, Arum, Crocus, Cyclamen, Fritillaria, Galanthus, Leucojum, Lilium, Muscari, Narcissus, Ornithogalum, Scilla* and *Tulipa* are among the most easily naturalized varieties.

• **Spring bulbs.** Although many wild species of bulbous plants bloom throughout the year, spring is without a doubt the classic bulb season. Spring begins with arrival of snowdrops (*Galanthus*), crocuses and *Eranthis*, continues with *Chionodoxa*, grape hyacinths *(Muscari)* and fritillaries and comes to a close with hyacinths. *Allium, Camassia, Cyclamen, Eremurus, Scilla* and the thousands of varieties of tulips are also among the many memorable spring bloomers.

• **Summer bulbs.** Most summer-blooming bulbs are too delicate to be naturalized and must, therefore, be planted in the spring when the danger of a late frost has passed. Some summer bulbs can only be planted outdoors in very warm climates.

Achimenes, Agapanthus, Amaryllis, Anemone, Canna, Crocosmia, Dahlia, Galtonia, Gladiolus, Gloriosa, Hymenocallis, Lilium, Oxalis, Sparaxis, Sprekelia, Tigridia, Tritonia and Zantedeschia are among the most popular summer bloomers.

• **Fall and winter bulbs**. In addition to the typical fall-blooming bulbs, like crocuses and Colchicum, some species in this category are able to keep their blooms up until the first frost; the best known and loved among these are undoubtedly the dahlias. Climate permitting, even during the coldest months of the year snow-drops, crocuses, cyclamen, and Eranthis can brighten up your garden, but winter is the ideal season for dedicating oneself to exotic plants that bloom only in a greenhouse or indoors, and

The lily is a typical summer bulb; its glorious multicolored flowers appear in July and August.

Both grape hyacinths (above) and ornamental onions (opposite page, top left) add a touch of class to any rock garden.

for concentrating on the fascinating technique of forcing bulbs.

Bulbs for rock gardens

The rock garden is the true delight of all garden lovers. In a very limited space it is possible to create very different growing conditions and cultivate a great number of species.

The following is a list of bulbs that grow well in rock gardens: *Allium, Anemone, Camassia, Chionodoxa, Corydalis, Crocus, Cyclamen, Eranthis, Fritallaria, Calanthus, Hyacinthus, Ixiolirion, Muscari, Ornithogalum, Oxalis, Pleione, Puschkinia, Scilla, Sprekelia* and *Tulipa.*

Cut flowers

Many bulbs produce flowers that are excellent for cutting and using in floral arrangements. If this procedure is performed with the help of a well-sharpened knife, without cutting off too many leaves, and

Below, a modern tulip and hyacinth farm.

At bottom, the tiny crocus also grows happily indoors in all types of containers.

possibly during the evening hours, there is no reason to fear doing damage to the plant. On the contrary, taking occasional cuttings helps the plant save its energy for seed production and maturation.

Allium, Crocosmia, Dahlia, Eremurus, Eucharis, Freesia, Iris, Ixia, Ixiolirion, Lilium, Narcissus, Nerine, Sparaxis and *Tulipa* make some of the best cut flowers.

Indoor flowers

By purchasing bulbs specifically designed to be "forced" (prematurely made to bloom indoors during the winter months), and by following the simple tech-

niques provided, you can enjoy beautiful flowers indoors during the holidays and year-round. Hyacinths, tulips, daffodils, irises, crocuses and scillas all respond marvelously to forcing.

STRUCTURAL CHARACTERISTICS

Many attempts have been made to individuate the environmental conditions that led to the evolution of bulbs, and in the process it has been discovered that that bulbous species are particularly able to adapt to satisfy very different ecological needs.

Many Asian tulips, for example, have adapted to a very extreme continental climate with brief, but heavy, spring rains and scorching, arid summers; while some fritillaries, on the other hand, have adapted to heavily saturated, marshy soil. There are also many species, like snowdrops and scillas, that are at home in the woodland underbrush. Because of their ability to store food, these species grow very rapidly and are able to complete their reproductive cycle at the beginning of spring, before the leaves of the deciduous trees are able to open and block their sun.

These differences exist, however, because the storage organs of bulbous plants differ tremendously in both structure and function.

Bulbs

Bulbs are a kind of complete plant in miniature. Bulbs are made up of a very short conical stem of leathery or coriaceous tissue, called a basal plate, from which the bud grows The bud is protected by modified, white, fleshy leaves, called scales, that contain the plant's stored food: starch, sugars and proteins. Slender, adventitious roots branch off from the basal plate. In many cases, bulbs are protected by a thin, papery layer of particular dry, brown, white or black leaves called the tunic. Bulbs, with a few rare exceptions (e.g., *Cardiocrinium*), are perennials and can, therefore, replenish their stored food from year to year. Grape hyacinths,

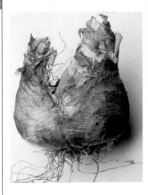

Despite their different shape and color, hyacinths (above) and daffodils (below) both grow from bulbs.

tulips, daffodils, lilies and ornamental onions (*Allium*) are all flowering bulbs.

Tubers

Tubers are underground storage organs made up of enlarged, modified stem tissue, almost entirely comprised of its stored nutrients. It lacks a tunic and its surface is covered with modified buds called "eyes," from which new shoots will sprout as soon as soon as the proper growing conditions are provided. *Cyclamen, Gloriosa, Anemone, Eranthis* and the begonia are all tubers.

Bulbs can be used to create of blocks of color that will brighten up any gray urban area.

Corms

Corms are similar to tubers, but with proportionately much more stem tissue. While bulbs use their modified leaves (scales) to store food, corms have smaller, thinner scales and their nutrients inside the fleshy stem, from the base of which the roots also branch off. One or two buds can be found, protected by the modified leaves, in the upper portion of the corm. These buds will grow into new plants. Unlike bulbs, corms exhaust their food storage every growing season and are transformed into dried disks from which they are able to completely regenerate themselves. Gladioli, crocuses, freesias and *Ixia* are all corms.

Rhizomes

Rhizomes are modified stems that grow horizontally, just below the

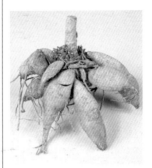

Above, from left to right: corm, tuberous root and tuber. By simply looking at the plants on the opposite page, it is not easy to tell which underground organ produces which plant.

surface. Leaves and flower stems grow on the upper side, while roots grow from the lower side. Anemones, lilies of the valley, calla lilies, cannas and *Agapanthus* are all rhizomes.

Tuberous Roots

Tuberous roots are modified roots that have been transformed in storage organs. They are no longer capable of absorbing nutrients and, therefore, need other roots to perform this function. The buds are generally located at the base of the stem. Some examples of flowers with tuberous roots: dahlias, *Ranunculus* and *Alstroemeria*.

REPRODUCTION

Although the biological cycles of plants are extremely diverse, they have all evolved towards the optimal performance of one single task: reproduction or, in other words, the preservation of the species.

The steps in this process are numerous. As soon as climate and humidity allow, bulbs, corms, tubers, rhizomes and tuberous roots leave the dormant state and begin to grow and reproduce. The root structure is usually the first to develop. It performs the double task of anchoring the plant in the ground and absorbing water and minerals from the soil.

Only when the roots have been firmly anchored does plant begin to grow up out of the soil. The aboveground parts of the plant are used for reproduction and the conversion of sunlight, water and carbon dioxide into the nutrients that the plant needs to grow (photosynthesis), including those that it will store for next year's growing season. For this reason, it is always better to wait as long as possible before digging up your bulbs.

If the climate is unfavorable, however, bulbs continue their subterranean existence utilizing their stored energy to create bulbils (small lateral bulbs that grow from the original "mother" bulb), or to create new scales inside the tunic. For reasons that still remain a mystery, some lilies and fritillaries can actually skip an entire reproductive cycle.

Besides fertilization—which occurs when the pollen, containing the male reproductive cells and located in the anthers, unites with the female ovules located in the pistil—plants are able to reproduce in another way, called agamic or vegetative propagation. In this case, the progeny is always identical to its one and only parent, and genetic material is not exchanged between plants. Vegetative propagation occurs spontaneously when a bulbil is detached from the mother plant and begins to live and grow autonomously. This phenomenon is readily evident in tulips and daffodils.

Some species of *Lilium* are able to produce small bulbs that appear at the leaf's axil (the angle between the stem and the leaf), that shortly after the plant has flowered detach from the mother plant and fall to the ground. If environmental conditions are favorable, these small bulbs will mature and be capable of flowering in one to two years.

Some species of tulips (e.g., *Tulipa sylvestris*) emit stolons from the base of the bulb that are able to reach 70 cm (28 in) in length, and at the end of which new bulbs are formed.

Rhizomes also have efficient reproductive structures. The iris, for example, invades its surrounding territory and from every node a new plant can grow.

Even the most delicate varieties can be grown almost anywhere with the help of containers (opposite). Containers can be moved indoors and outdoors to artificially recreate the required climatic conditions not naturally provided by the local climate. Even lilies (below) can be grown in containers, as well as in the garden.

Above, Asiatic lilies and other varieties of flowering bulbs can be grown in wooden crates. Below, cross-section of a bulb; the developing bud is highly visible.

CULTIVATION

Buying bulbs

Buying bulbs is not difficult. The most common varieties are easily found in gardening stores, nurseries or even in department stores, while the less common varieties can be mail-ordered or ordered online from specialized bulb companies. In all cases, but especially if the distributor offers low prices and no money-back guarantee, it is a good idea to keep the following golden rules in mind. Bulbs or corms must always be whole, with no signs of damage by insects or other organisms. They must also be compact, firm and reasonably heavy—a light bulb may be the sign of damage or dehydration. Before making large purchases, it is always a good idea to cut one bulb from each new batch in half to make sure that the batch is healthy.

After you have acquired your bulbs, it is a good idea to plant them as soon as possible, especially if they have not been well packed or stored. Bulbs with protective tunics, like hyacinths, daffodils and tulips, can be stored in shallow containers for some time.

Tubers (e.g., cyclamen), bulbs without tunics (e.g., lilies, fritillaries) or bulbs with fleshy, persistent roots (e.g., irises) can become easily dehydrated and should not remain exposed for long periods of time. If necessary, they can be stored for brief periods in containers filled with sand or moist peat.

Preparing the Soil

The planting area must be thoroughly tilled and raked. All large rocks should be removed along with any stray roots, and hard clumps of earth should be broken up. Most bulbs require a light, loamy soil, or a rich, slightly sandy soil with good drainage.

"Light soil," the opposite of "heavy soil," does not refer to the soil's actual weight, but defines how easy it is to work. "Texture" refers to the size of the individual soil particles. Fine soil can contain, in varying proportions, coarse and fine gravel, coarse and fine sand, silt and claylike substances. Each category has been determined based on the particles' dimensions, in descending order.

Sandy soil is 70–80 percent sand, clay soil is more than 25–30 percent clay and loamy soil—the ideal soil from an agronomic point of view—is 45–80 percent sand, 10–15 percent silt, 5–10 percent clay, 1–5 percent limestone and 3–5 percent organic matter.

The porosity, on the other hand, is measured by the percentage of pores and interstices present in the soil. Medium porosity is reached at approximately 50 percent. Sandy soil is 30–40 percent porous, clay soil is 55–60 percent porous and loamy soil is 70–80 percent porous.

A few simple gardening tools, such as gloves, a garden trowel and a bulb planter are highly recommended.

Another important characteristic is the ability of rainwater or water from artificial sources to permeate the soil without causing the topsoil to erode; this usually occurs when the soil is heavy, compact or perhaps even impermeable.

Very few bulbs, besides callas and water lilies, require or even tolerate soil where water accumulates easily. With clay soils, it may be necessary to correct the soil with sand, manure or a loam of leaves to aid drainage, and in some cases it may be a good idea to dig irrigation canals. In desperate cases, small areas can be planted using imported soil, kept separate with underground dividers.

Fertilizers

Plants use their roots to extract the moisture and minerals they need to grow from the soil. These minerals are comprised of 12 essential elements. Some of these elements, namely boron, manganese, copper, zinc and molybdenum, the so-called "micro elements" (or micro nutrients) are consumed in infinitesimal quantities and are only present in the composition of some enzymes. Plants are very rarely deficient in these elements. Calcium, magnesium, sulfur, iron, nitrogen, phosphorous and potassium, however, are considered structural or macro elements (also called macronutrients) and are essential to the plant's survival.

Nitrogen comprises 1–3 percent of the dry weight of the plant's mature tissue and 5–6 percent of its young tissue. It is an important element in the composition of protein, chlorophyll, nucleic acid (which determines the plant's hereditary characteristics) and other essential substances like alkaloids and glycosides. It is consumed only in its mineral state, and in large quantities during reproduction, with peak consumption during periods of root development and during the formation of the reproductive organs. It should be added regularly to any soil that is cultivated on a regular basis.

	CLASS	PARTICLE SIZE	
Stones and Gravel	Stones and pebbles	> 10 mm	(> 0.39 in)
	Coarse gravel	5–10 mm	(0.2–0.39 in)
	Fine gravel	2–5 mm	(0.08–0.2 in)
Fine earth	Coarse sand	2–0.2 mm	(0.08–0.008 in)
	Fine sand	0.2–0.02 mm	(0.008–0.0008 in)
	Silt	0.02–0.002 mm	(0.0008–0.00008 in)
	Clay	< 0.002 mm	(< 0.00008 in)

Fertilizer is essential for growing strong, healthy plants both in the garden and in containers, as long as it is applied as recommended.

Nitrogen can be administered in its mineral form using calcium cynamide, urea, ammonium sulfate, anhydrous ammonia, calcium nitrate or ammonium nitrate. The best time to perform this task is generally during the spring, so as to coincide with the beginning of the new growing season. This is the time of year when plants are most in need of this nutrient and its presence in the soil is usually scarce, because the biological processes that take place during the mineralization of organic substances have only just begun. Nitrogen-rich soil favors growth and leaf development, but can be detrimental if too generously applied.

Phosphorus also plays an important role in the plant's life cycle from the moment it enters the nucleic acids of the molecules responsible for photosynthesis and energy exchange. It is also one of the most important substances stored in seeds, tubers, etc. Phosphorus stimulates and accelerates the phenomena linked to flowering, fertilization and fruit matura-tion. Phosphorus fertilizer has no known risks, and can be adminis-tered with phosphate minerals such as single superphosphate, triple superphosphate, bone meal, rock phosphate, colloidal phosphate or so-called "Thomas dross," the dross collected in Thomas Converters during the steel refining process and which are finely ground and sold as phosphate fertilizer.

Potassium, which comprises 1 percent of the dry weight of the plant's organic tissues, plays a key role in all of the mechanisms that regulate the cell membrane's semipermeability, the plant's pH, the formation and accumulation of nutrients, and the resistance to damage caused by the cold or other adversities. A well-balanced potassium fertilization can be accomplished using potassium chloride (muriate of potash), potassium sulfate or potassium nitrate and contributes to the strengthening of the plant's stems and improves the perfume and color of its flowers and general health of the plant.

Often, for the sake of convenience, mineral fertilizers are not singularly administered, but in a mixture of two or three different elements. Generally a series of numbers, following the name of the mixture, indicates its principal components. These numbers are known as NPK ratios. The first number indicates the percentage of nitrogen, the second that of phosphorus and the third that of potassium. Therefore the numbers 6-12-6 represent 6 percent nitrogen, 12 percent phosphorus and 6 percent potassium. Leaf fertilizers, made to be absorbed directly from leaves, can also be found on the market. Besides nitrogen, phosphorus and potassium, these products can also contain microelements that may prove to be very useful in situations where the soil has been generally depleted by periods of severe weather (cold, draught, etc.).

Small quantities of slow dissolving granular fertilizer can be mixed into the soil when the bulbs are planted, as with these daffodils illustrated above.

Organic Fertilizers

While, when done correctly, the spreading of mineral fertilizers will have an immediate positive effect on the growth and health of your plants, successful gardening over long periods of time is inextricably linked to the presence of organic matter in the soil.

In natural environments, unaltered by human intervention, plant and animal remains are returned to the earth, where with the help of many organisms and microorganisms, they decompose and are biochemically transformed into a blackish, amorphous substance that can not be broken down any further, known as humus. This substance has a beneficial effect on the soil's physical and chemical

Many bulbs grow better when the soil (top) has been amended with peat (bottom) and sand.

characteristics as well as its structure, porosity and workability. Also, as humus slowly becomes mineralized it releases precisely those mineral elements that are so indispensable to the growth of plants. In nature, organic matter is naturally returned to the soil, but in soil that has been cultivated—especially where the product is harvested and removed—organic matter must be deliberately re-introduced. However, not all organic supplements have the same effects. Organic matter that is rich in lignin and cellulose, like straw, has a positive effect on a plant's structure, but not on its nutrition, since it is not easily mineralized and has little nitrogen. Moisture-rich substances like grass and leaves, on the other hand, mineralize quickly and, therefore, provide nutrients that are readily assimilated by plants. In any case, there are many useful organic fertilizers available. Those most widely used in floriculture are well-rotted manure, compost, peat and blood meal. Well-rotted or decomposed manure is an excellent fertilizer that is a mixture of animal excrement and materials produced when the manure is left to ferment for several months. During this fermentation period the manure is slowly transformed into a uniform, odorless black paste. Only when it has reached this state should it be used as fertilizer. Manure is generally spread during the fall so that it is already highly decomposed by the following spring at the start of the new growing season.

Compost is another good fertilizer and one that can be readily produced by anyone, using everyday kitchen scraps and yard clippings.

Peat is partly carbonized vegetable matter of natural origin that has accumulated over the centuries in particular acid substrata (peat bogs) characterized by their lack of oxygen and excessive humidity. Peat is generally used in container growing because of its ability to retain water and provide structure to the soil.

Fertilizers consisting partially of blood meal are also very effective for their high nitrogen content that is released gradually into the soil. This kind of fertilizer, however, is completely lacking in phosphorus.

Amending the soil

The soil's acidity affects the life and health of plants. The presence of nutrients in the soil, and the activity of microorganisms, responsible for the mineralization of the organic matter, vary tremendously depending on the acidity or alkalinity of the substrate, and in many cases it may be necessary or helpful to amend it. The easiest way to amend acidic soil is by adding calcium carbonate, lime or marl in various doses according to the situation. Excessive alkalinity, on the other hand, can be corrected by administering a little chalk (calcium sulfate) or sulfur.

It may be also be necessary to further intervene by modifying the soil's physical characteristics (e.g., structure or texture). Adding organic matter is usually the easiest way to amend both soil that is overly loose or overly compact. The addition of sand can also be used in restricted areas to improve the soil's texture and to amend clay soil. Calcium is also always good for the soil.

Planting

Planting bulbs is relatively simple, and the rules are elementary and few. In most cases a universal soil mixed with sand and peat can be used. The correct proportion is 20 percent sand, 30 percent peat and the remaining 50 percent soil. As far as specific planting depths for the different species of bulbs, tubers and rhizomes are concerned, please refer to the individual species descriptions found in the following chapters. Generally speaking, however, bulbs should be planted deeper in dry, sandy soil and less deep in heavy, clay soil. But, it is always safer, however, to err on the side of too deep rather than too shallow. Another general rule of thumb is to plant bulbs at a depth that equals two to three times their greatest diameter. The spacing between bulbs also varies widely depending on the desired effect, but for natural looking groupings of crocuses, snowdrops or cyclamens, plant bulbs 5–10 cm (2–4 in) apart. Larger species like gladioli, hyacinths, irises and lilies should be spaced at 30 cm (12 in) or more.

When and how

When to plant your bulbs depends largely on their blooming season: spring-blooming bulbs (tulips, daffodils, lilies-of-the-valley, fritillaries, etc.) must be planted in the fall, while summer-blooming bulbs (calla lilies, dahlias, lilies, gladioli, etc.) must be planted in the spring.

How to plant your bulbs, on the other hand, depends largely on the number bulbs you wish to plant: if you only have a few bulbs, prepare a gardening palate with freshly turned soil. The area should be workable enough to permit the easy extraction of small cylinders of soil of the required depth. These cylinders will be replaced after the bulbs have been planted. For a larger quantity of bulbs, remove a rectangular patch of soil of the desired depth and dimension (according to bulb type and quantity) using a planting spade. In the prepared rectangle,

TYPE OF MANURE	NITROGEN	PHOSPHORUS	POTASSIUM
Well-rotted mixed manure	5.0	2.6	5.3
Horse manure	6.7	2.3	7.2
Cow manure	3.4	1.3	3.5
Pig manure	4.5	2.0	6.0
Sheep manure	8.2	2.1	8.4

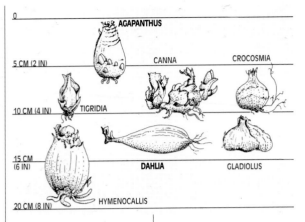

0			
	AGAPANTHUS		
5 CM (2 IN)		CANNA	CROCOSMIA
10 CM (4 IN)	TIGRIDIA		
15 CM (6 IN)		**DAHLIA**	GLADIOLUS
20 CM (8 IN)	HYMENOCALLIS		

These two tables illustrate the required planting depths for the most common bulbs.

32

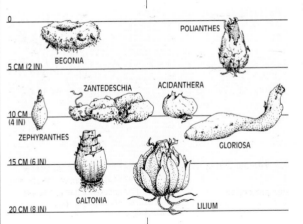

0			
			POLIANTHES
5 CM (2 IN)	BEGONIA		
	ZANTEDESCHIA	ACIDANTHERA	
10 CM (4 IN)			
ZEPHYRANTHES			GLORIOSA
15 CM (6 IN)			
	GALTONIA		
20 CM (8 IN)		LILIUM	

sprinkle bone meal and cover it with a thin layer of soil, arrange bulbs as desired (keeping in mind their spacing requirements) and cover. This method is not difficult and yields excellent results.

Container growing

Even without a garden you can still surround yourself with beautiful flowering bulbs with the help of flowerpots and window boxes. Planting season, depth and spacing should remain the same, but more careful attention must be paid to drainage. To avoid poor drainage, use clay pots or place a layer of pebbles or clay at the bottom of the container. Obviously, small to medium sized plants are best suited to container growing because they generally require less soil. However, nothing should stop you from growing taller plants if the adequate size container is used.

Irrigation

Only a true expert is able to keep track of how much water a plant requires in its different growth stages. However, generally speaking, plants are most in need of water when they are in bloom, especially if this occurs during the summer months, like with lilies, gladioli and dahlias. Also, keep in mind that plants grown in containers become more easily dehydrated because the soil dries more rapidly. Emergency irrigation may be necessary in dry seasons for hardy spring-bloomers.

Also, bulbs can not be neglected after they have bloomed. Rapid dehydration of the leaves prematurely interrupts photosynthesis, which can cause nutrient deficiency during the next growth season. This can easily be avoided, however, by following a few simple rules: water should always be air temperature and should never have too much lime. The pressure of the hose or irrigation system should also not create a violent jet of water that will shift the soil and expose the roots, or do direct damage to the

plant itself. During the summer, avoid watering during the hottest hours of the day.

End of the growth season and winter protection

All experienced gardeners know that flowers should be removed as soon as they begin to wilt. This practice saves the plant the considerable energy it would otherwise spend in seed production.

Another important rule, and one that is often ignored, is to avoid damaging or cutting back the plant's leaf structure until the leaves have completely withered. Only when the leaves are allowed to wither naturally is the plant able to store enough food to last it until the

When planting different types of bulbs together (above, daffodils and Chionodoxa) be sure to take into consideration both their colors as well as their blooming periods, which can be made to coincide, or staggered sequentially.

The amount of water that a plant requires varies greatly depending on its location. This crate of dahlias, placed under a tree and surrounded by many other plants requires much less water than if it were placed on a sunny deck or balcony.

next growth season. Plants also consume large amounts of energy during flower production, which is only replenished during photosynthesis.

At the end of the growth season, all that remains for the gardener to do is to plan for the inclement months ahead. However, not all plants are able to tolerate cold winters. The hardier spring bulbs, like crocuses, daffodils, tulips and scillas, and many of the other "classic bulbs" are able to withstand lows of up to -20°C (-4°F), but the less hardy species, must be protected during the winter (unless the local climate is particularly mild year-round). This can be accomplished by covering the ground with a winter mulch of dry leaves, straw, wood chips or other materials to prevent the covered area from freezing underground. This area must be uncovered slowly towards the end of the winter, to prevent the soil from warming up too quickly and causing the bulbs to bloom prematurely.

Storing bulbs

So far we have focused on bulbs (and there are many) that can be left in the soil year-round, but there are some more delicate bulbs like *Acidanthera, Crinum, Crocosmia, Gloriosa* and *Tigridia* that must be extracted from the soil and stored until the following spring. Once bulbs have been extracted from the soil, they must be wiped clean, treated with a fungicide and left to dry for 10 days in a well-ventilated area. They should then be stored in open, shallow, wooden boxes filled with peat or vermiculite. Bulbs should also be spaced well apart so as to keep any eventual rotting that may occur from spreading. It is also a good idea to cover the box with some kind of wire mesh to keep out mice or other rodents. Tuberous roots (dahlias) should be stored at about 6°C (43°F), *Achimenes* at 13°C (55°F) and tropical species at 17°C (63°F).

Bulbs that have been cultivated indoors do not need to be immediately removed from their containers as long as you are careful to stop watering them as soon as the leaves have turned brown. When this occurs, the containers can be stored until the following season in an area where the bulbs will not freeze. At the start of the new growth season, the bulbs must be removed from their containers, wiped clean, sprinkled with fungicidal powder and replanted with new soil.

The storage temperature of bulbs varies greatly from one genus to the next. The tuberous roots of dahlias should be stored at 5–7 °C (41–45 °F).

PROPAGATION

There are two types of propagation: vegetative (agamic) or by seed (gamic).

Propagation by seed (gamic)

Gamic propagation (or sexual reproduction) occurs when the pollen (containing the male cells) located on the anthers, is united with ovules (the female cells) located in the ovary. The reproductive process unfolds as follows: pollen is carried from the anthers (located at the tip of the stamens) to the stigma (the opening of the female reproductive organ) by the wind, bees or other insects. Once deposited on the stigma, the male cells make their way down through the style (the tube that connects the stigma to the ovary) to the ovary, where the ovules are located, to complete fertilization. At this point, a series of complex phenomena are set in motion and seeds (embryos supplied with a store of nutrients and wrapped in a protective integument) are produced. Seeds come in all different shapes and sizes and are sometimes protected by a fruit.

The continual mixing together of genetic material during fertilization is what causes diversity within the species and is also the basis for evolution. In floriculture, the constant modification of a species' characteristics, caused by sexual reproduction, is only desired when a new variety is being created, otherwise it is generally preferred that the different species or varieties of plants stay the same for as long as possible. This is accomplished with agamic or vegetative propagation. New plants created with vegetative propagation are always genetically identical to their only parent. Bulb lovers also usually do not like to use seeds to create new plants because most bulbous plants obtained from seeds do not flower until the plant is four to five years old, or older: *Cardiocrinum giganteum,* for example does not start flowering until it is seven years old. There are a few exceptions, however. Mignon dahlias, for example, planted in February or March will bloom that same year, and freesias only take 6–12 months to flower.

The ability of seeds to survive varies greatly and, depending on species and the way in which they are stored, seeds can maintain themselves, unaltered, for days, months or even years. In order to germinate, however, certain levels of oxygen and humidity and temperature must be provided. Seeds are usually not planted directly in the ground but in wooden, plastic or clay containers of various dimensions with a layer of pebbles, sand or broken pieces of terracotta on the bottom to ensure proper drainage. Seeds should ideally be planted in a soil that is equal parts peat, sand and potting soil. Seeds that have a very hard seed coat (e.g., freesias) should be soaked for 24 hours before planting. Generally speaking, small seeds can simply be sprinkled on top of the soil, while larger seeds should be covered with a layer of soil or sand that is equal to their diameter.

Buying new bulbs is not the only way to obtain beautiful new blooms (like those on the opposite page). In many varieties, the mother bulb spontaneously produces new bulbs (bulbils), which can be separated to create new plants. These daffodils (above) are just one of the many examples.

Seeds should be watered frequently, using a watering can with very fine holes so as to create a shower effect. For best results, a constant level of humidity should be maintained. This can be obtained by covering the seed containers with a thick damp cloth or a sheet of glass, which should be removed as soon as the seeds begin

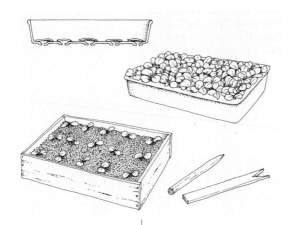

In the above illustration, an example of seed propagation. The bottom of the tray is covered in broken pieces of clay flowerpots to facilitate drainage; the small plants are later repotted in larger containers.

to germinate. Germination usually occurs anywhere from a few days to a few weeks after planting. *Lilium auratum,* however, takes up to three months to sprout! The ideal growing temperature is 14–18°C (57–64°F). When the young plants are large enough to be easily handled, they can be replanted in larger containers filled with potting soil and spaced 3–5 cm (1–2 in) apart. Special care must be taken so as not to damage their roots or small stems. At this point, depending on species, plants can either be kept indoors or in a greenhouse for a while longer, or planted directly in the garden.

Vegetative propagation (agamic)

This is the most widely used method of bulb propagation. It is also the method that is used to obtain new plants that are genetically identical to the "mother plant." Normally, mature bulbs and corms

develop small bulbs or "bulbils" around their base that can be detached from the mother bulb to produce new plants. Bulbils must be harvested in the fall and stored during the winter in a dry location; they can be planted in containers in the spring, where they will grow until they have reached the necessary flowering dimensions. Gladiolus corms, for example, produce numerous pea-sized bulbils that will produce flowers in two to three years. These bulbils or "cormels" should be planted in mid-March, 30 cm (12 in) apart and 10 cm (4 in) deep, in potting soil, between two layers of sand. Many lilies produce two or more bulbils every year that can be separated from the mother bulb in the fall or in the spring. Tulips produce three different sized bulbils: small, medium and large. The largest type should be planted at a depth of 15 cm (6 in), while the other two at depths of 5–10 cm (2–4 in). They should also be placed at a distance that is double their size. They will flower in one (the largest type) to three years (the smaller ones).

Some species of *Lilium*, such as *L. bulbiferum, L. tigrinum* and *L. sargentiae* produce blackish purple or green "axillary buds" located at the leaf axil. Axillary buds can be detached in August or September when the leaves begin to yellow, and planted in small flowerpots. In one to two years they should be large enough to start producing blooms.

Some kinds of ornamental onions (*Allium*) produce "aerial bulbils," located on the umbels, that can be treated in the same way as those produced by lilies. The corms of some members of the *Iridaceae* family (e.g., gladioli and crocuses) can be divided to produce new plants. In this case, the corm must be cut vertically with a well-sharpened knife, making sure that each half contains at least one bud and one section of the basal plate. The cut surface should then be covered with fungicide. It can be planted when the cut surface has dried.

Tubers and rhizomes can be propagated by simply dividing their underground organs, as long as each piece contains at least one to two buds. This can be done with the rhizomes of calla lilies, cannas, irises, *Hedychium* and *Smithiantha*, and the tubers of the *Gloriosa*.

On the opposite page, Asiatic and calla lilies. Below, cannas are beginning to sprout.

These are all plants that perform vegetative propagation, beginning with the bulbs and rhizomes of the mother plant.

39

The tuberous roots of dahlias, on the other hand, are much more difficult to divide because their buds are located only at the neck or "collet" and, therefore, must be divided so that each cut portion contains at least one piece of stem of the mother plant. It is always a good idea to conclude these operations by treating the newly divided bulbs with a fungicidal powder to prevent any eventual pathogenous outbreaks.

The drawing below illustrates different types of vegetative propagation: (1) tuberous roots, (2) elongated rhizomes, (3–4) bulbils that form at the base of a bulb or corm and (5) scales.

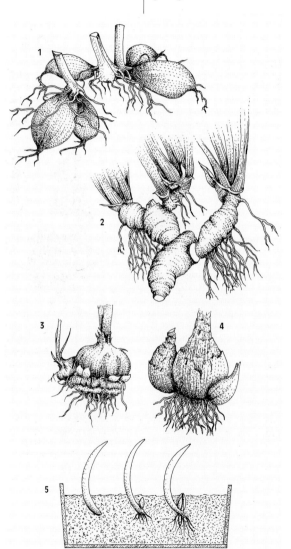

Furthermore, all species of lilies, along with their cultivars, can be propagated by delicately dividing the scales present in each bulb as long as a section of basal plate is left on each section. For best results, plant scales at a slight angle in containers filled with an equal mixture of peat and sand and cover them only halfway. New bulbs will soon form at the base of each scale. This operation can be performed in spring or autumn and the ideal temperature for the most successful propagation is 10–12°C (50–54°F). Irrigation should also be gradually increased as the roots and bulbils begin to grow.

Dahlias and tuberous begonias can also be propagated by taking shoot cuttings. This relatively simple technique is great way to produce many new plants in a short period of time: plant the tubers or tuberous roots in damp peat and wait for them to sprout; when they are about 7–8 cm (2½ to 3 in) in length, new shoots can be separated and placed in an equal mixture of potting soil, peat and sand where they will begin to root.

Some plants in the *Gesneriaceae* family can also be propagated by leaf cuttings. In this case, in May or June, detach the leaves with buds, immerse them in a

mixture of sand and peat and maintain a constant temperature of 20–24°C (68–75°F). New sprouts will soon appear.

Above, these splendid gladioli are one of the many types of flowering bulbs that can be propagated by means of the cormels that form on the mother corm.

The illustration at left presents the different phases of development of an amaryllis grown in a container, and the illustration below depicts the development of a hyacinth forced to bloom in a carafe of water (or hyacinth glass).

INDOOR BULBS

Holiday bulbs

Fill your home with dazzling hyacinths, tulips, irises, crocuses and scillas even during the winter months by forcing bulbs to bloom indoors. Bulbs can be forced to bloom when the conditions that normally occur during their blooming season are artificially provided. By controlling a bulb's exposure to temperature, light and humidity, its natural biological rhythms can be accelerated and "forced" into action out of season.

There are two common ways to force bulbs. The first and easiest method is to purchase bulbs that have already been prepared for winter blooming. These bulbs have spent the summer in refrigerated storage and have, therefore, already experienced a "false winter" that corresponds to the cold season that their natural growth cycle requires. These types of "prepared" bulbs can simply be planted indoors

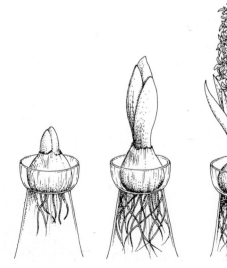

Cultivation in glass containers lets us enjoy our bulbs twice as long, because it allows us to view every stage of their growth.

immediately where they will soon grow and bloom. If growing prepared bulbs in water, the false winter must be prolonged for a brief period by blocking the light with a cardboard cone until the bulb begins to grow.

The second method uses normal, nonprepared bulbs. These bulbs must be planted in the fall, in wide shallow containers filled with potting soil, sand and peat, with the pointed end of the bulb left poking up out of the soil. The bulbs should then be watered and kept in a dark location at less than 10°C (50°F).

They can also be planted in a large container in the garden, buried in ash, peat or sand to keep them from freezing. This first phase, lasting a few months, will stimulate the formation of roots and leaves. When the leaves are about 3–4 cm (1–1½ in) in length, they can be transplanted and placed in a brightly lit location at about 10°C (50°F). After 10 to 15 days, when the leaves are about 10 cm (4 in) in length, the containers can be moved indoors where they will soon flower. Keep in mind, however, that even indoors they should be kept in a relatively cool location, at about 12–18°C (54–64°F) and away from any sources of heat, direct sun or draft. They must also be watered regularly and abundantly.

Growing bulbs in water

Some flowering bulbs (e.g. daffodils, hyacinths, grape hyacinths, crocuses and tulips) can be grown in water. This method is similar to growing in soil, and beautiful results can be obtained by following a few easy steps. For best results, choose a glass vase that is approxi-

mately 10 cm (4 in) wide and 15–25 cm (6–10 in) tall with a narrow neck that will support the bulb, but allow it to root in the water. After four to five weeks in a cool storage place (hyacinths must also be kept in the dark, but daffodils can be kept in the light), when the roots are about 7–10 cm (3–4 in) long and the leaves have begun to appear, transfer them indoors, where they will soon begin to bloom. This method produces excellent results, but exhausts the bulbs of their food store so that they can not be reused.

Delicate bulbs

Some of the more delicate, mostly tropical, species can not survive the winter outdoors and must, therefore, be planted in the spring for summer bloom-ing. These delicate bulbs also grow well in greenhouses or indoors. The amaryllis (*Hippeas-*

trum) is a typical example of this type of bulb, and if bulbs are planted gradually from October to March, they will be in bloom for the entire winter. *Hippeastrum* bulbs are very large and only one bulb should be planted per 12–15 cm (5–6 in) flowerpot. The bulb should be covered only halfway with a mixture of peat, sand, potting soil and ground limestone and watered immediately. Water again once they have begun to sprout and add a liquid fertilizer once a week throughout the entire growing season. Avoid placing them in direct sun. The leaves will generally last longer than the bloom and should continue to be watered regularly even after the bloom has withered. *Lachenalia, Nerine* and *Sprekelia* can also be planted this way, but in groups of six or more bulbs per container, with only the tips left uncovered. These bulbs they can be left in the same container for two years (except freesias and *Lachenalia*), longer for *Nerine*.

Equally beautiful flowers can be obtained from both the more delicate varieties of bulbs that must be cultivated indoors and the more hardy outdoor varieties.

PESTS AND DISEASES

Like all living organisms, bulbs are also are often the victim of parasites, mostly in the form of insects, mites, nematodes, molluscs and fungal, viral and bacterial diseases. Bulbs can also contract non-parasitic diseases.

GARDEN PESTS

Aphids are insects belonging to the Homoptera order. They live in large colonies and attack many kinds of plants, sucking out their sap. They can cause, depending on the species, sprout damage, leaf roll or galls. They also help spread viruses and emit a sweet, sticky substance called "honeydew" on which "sooty mold" soon develops.

• To control: In the case of an initial attack acephate, dimethoate or pyrethrins can be applied. For more advanced attacks, you will need a product that is able to penetrate plant tissue and strike aphid colonies protected by galls and leaf roll.

Ghost moths (*Hepialus humuli*). The larvae of these Lepidoptera are 2–4 cm (1–2 in) long and white with a black head. They tunnel into the roots of many plants, especially lilies-of-the-valley and *Alstroemeria*.

• To control: These pests can be kept at bay by frequently turning the soil.

Lily leaf beetles (*Lilioceris lilii*) are coleopterous insects of the Chrysomelidae family with coral red elytra (hard outer wing cases) in their larval state. They attack and gnaw the leaves of lilies, lilies-of-the-valley and fritillaries and hibernate at the adult stage.

• To control: Treat plants with carbaryl (Sevin).

Narcissus flies (or bulb maggots) (*Eumerus strigatus*). The adult of this species deposits its eggs on the collet of flowering bulbs. The larvae then invade the underground organs, burrowing into the bulbs, corms, tubers or rhizomes of many ornamental plants, like lilies, irises, gladioli, daffodils, hyacinths, etc.

Tulips are subject to frequent attacks by aphids and mites, these can be prevented by fumigating the bulbs.

• To control: The bulbs can be disinfested by immersing them in water at 45°C (113°F) for one hour.

Nematodes (*Anguillula*) are menacing microscopic worms that can invade many different kinds of plants, causing root swelling or stem and leaf deformation. One of the most common species is the eel worm (*Ditylencus dipasci*). They attack many species of plants, especially daffodils and hyacinths, causing black spots to appear inside the bulb and on the leaves. It also causes the flowers to wilt and small knotty growths to appear on the roots. There is also a kind of eel worm that attacks the root system of cyclamens

Gladioli are constantly attacked by click beetles, thrips and aphids. Fortunately there are many products available to help combat these garden pests.

and begonias, provoking root nodosity.

• To control: Disinfest the soil with a nematocide (e.g., Clandosan) and either remove and destroy the diseased plants, or treat plants when the first signs appear. It is also not a good idea to repeat the same kind of cultivation in infested soil.

Snails and slugs. Polyphagous and nocturnal snails (*Helix*) and slugs (*Limax*) devour the tender aboveground parts of the plant, especially when the weather is particularly humid. Although they are not picky eaters, they seem to have a penchant for lilies and dahlias. The silvery trail of slime that they leave behind is a sure sign of their presence.

• To control: Place metaldehyde bait near the plants you wish to protect.

Spider mites. These mites, belonging to the arachnid class, are miniscule creatures no bigger than a pinhead. They are equipped with a mosquito-like sucking organ, which they use to repeatedly puncture the leaves of many kinds of plants and suck out their sap. They multiply rapidly.

• To control: Miticides like tetradifon can be used.

Thrips are tiny insects belonging to the Thysanoptera order. They possess piercing-and-sucking mouth parts, which they use to suck the sap out of the leaves and petals on which they feed, causing silvery spots, deformations, petal drop and stunted leaf growth. Greenhouse thrips (*Heliothrips haemorrhoidalis*) usually attack flowering greenhouse plants, while the gladiolus thrips (*Taeniothrips simplex*) infest the corms, leaves and flowers of the gladiolus. They hibernate inside the corms, making them black and sticky.

Lilies have their own personal enemies; this coleopteran is called the "lily leaf beetle," but it also attacks lilies-of-the-valley and fritillaries.

48

• To control: Thrips can be combated using phosphorus insecticides or carbamide. In any case, always check that the corms are healthy before planting, especially with gladioli. They can be disinfested by immersing them in 45°C (113°F) water for about 30 minutes.

Voles and mice. Both voles and mice seem to possess a true predilection for bulbs, corms and tubers and crocuses seem to be among one of the most appetizing species.
• To control: Zinc phosphide or coumarin-based rodenticides can be used, or try placing a wire cage around bulbs.

Water lily leaf beetles (*Galerucella nymphaeae*). The larvae of these coleopterous insects drill holes in the leaves of water lilies (*Nymphaea*) and spatterdock (*Nuphar*).
• To control: The best way to control is by removing the larvae infested leaves. Phosphates can also be used, but these can seep into the ground water and damage the environment.

Whiteflies (*Trialeurodes vaporariorum*) are homopterous insects of tropical origin, similar to tiny white butterflies. These common greenhouse pests suck the sap from many types of plants, including the gladiolus.
• To control: Whiteflies can be combated using a dimethoate-based product.

Wireworms (*Agriotes lineatus*) are the larval stage of click beetles and are characterized by their elongated cylindrical form and leathery yellow skin. They live in the soil and tunnel into and feed on bulbs, tubers and roots.
• To control: These are usually only a problem in new gardens and can be eliminated by keeping the soil well turned and by planting where there is good drainage. Also, beneficial nematodes can be used.

BULB DISEASES

Black leg disease (*Pectobacterium carotovorum*). This bacteria, spread by the larva of certain Lepidoptera, causes the nauseating putrefaction of rhizomes and the spontaneous dehydration of the leaves.
• To control: Disinfect rhizomes with copper sulfate before planting.

While the "narcissus fly" and the "whitefly" attack gladioli, "mealybugs" sometimes attack the foliage of begonias.

49

To prevent the roots of calla lilies from rotting (pictured above, in a charming wicker basket), its rhizomes should be disinfested before planting.

Blue mold (*Penicillium*) is a type of fungus that can appear as a blue-green mold on bulbs, corms or tubers when they are in storage.

• To control: Blue mold can be prevented by storing bulbs, tubers and corms in a well-ventilated and dry location. If it does occur, treat with captan.

Bulb rot. This term is used to define various fungal diseases in the *Fusarium* genus. Bulb rot tends to strike in warm, humid climates and in acid soil with poor drainage. It attacks many species, including crocuses, cyclamens, gladioli, daffodils and lilies, generally causing bulbs and corms to rot and the plant to wilt.

• To control: Bulb rot can generally be prevented by correctly amending the soil and choosing resistant varieties.

Cyclamen anthracnose (*Cryptocline cyclaminis*), very widespread in greenhouse cultivation, causes the new growth of tubers to rot and the stems (and sometimes leaves and flowers) to become covered with oval-shaped pockmarks.

• To control: Treat with a dithiocarbamate fungicide as soon as the first symptoms appear.

Gladiolus dry rot (*Stromatinia gladioli*) is a fungus that attacks gladioli, crocuses, freesias and *Acidanthera,* causing very tiny black masses to appear around the collet, turning leaves dry and yellow and damaging the corm structure.

• To control: This fungus can be prevented by using healthy bulbs and corms.

Gray mold (*Botrytis*) causes spots to appear on the plant's leaves, flowers and bulbs. Attacks can be especially violent during rainy periods. If the plant is severely afflicted, it will become covered with a dense even layer of gray mold. Tulips, gladioli and hyacinths are just a few examples of the many types of bulbs that can contract this disease.

• To control: It can largely be prevented by making sure to choose healthy bulbs with no visible lesions. It can be treated with a vinclozolin-based fungicide.

Scab (neck rot). Different species of bacteria attack flowering bulbs. *Pseudomonas marginata* and *Pseudomonas hyacinthi*, for example, cause numerous tiny brown spots to appear on the leaves (in hyacinths) and circular lesions on the corms.

• To control: The best way to combat is through prevention, which consists of the disinfestation of the soil and the planting of healthy specimens.

Sclerotinia dry rot (*Sclerotinia gladioli*) is a fungus that attacks the leaves and stems of crocuses and gladioli, making them turn yellow and dry. Large rotting lesions also appear on the corms.

• To control: The only way to control is by destroying the diseased plants and moving the garden to a new plot.

Sclerotinia rot (*Sclerotinia tuliparum*) is a fungus that usually attacks tulips and hyacinths in the form of a gray mold and causes the breakdown of plant tissues.

• To control: Destroy all sick plants and disinfest the soil and bulbs with a phthalimide fungicide before planting.

Septoriosis is a fungal disease belonging to the *Septoria* genus. It usually spreads with humid weather and is particularly feared in the greenhouse. It causes leaf spotting. With gladioli, spots also appear on the corms.

• To control: Treat with a phthalimide fungicide or copper sulfate as soon as the first symptoms appear

Soft rot is caused by different types of fungi (e.g., *Sclerotinia sclerotiorum* and *Botrytis gladiolorum*) that attack hyacinth bulbs, *Acidanthera* corms and the tuberous roots of dahlias while in storage, causing them to rot and turn black.

• To control: Store bulbs, corms and tubers in cool, well ventilated areas.

Rust is a fungus that causes small reddish-brown pustules to appear either in clusters, or singularly on the leaves of irises and other plants. It usually only causes limited damage.

The perfection of this trumpet daffodil is reassuring: the healthy plant is the norm, the unhealthy plant is the exception.

The begonia (below) and the crocus (above) are both prone to bacteriosis and septoriosis.

- To control: Use resistant varieties.

Viruses are caused by extremely small, noncellular, viral organisms. Symptoms include: green or yellow streaks or blotches, patchy discoloration, dwarfism and, in some cases, the formation of growths, pustules and leaf deformation. Viruses can strike crocuses, dahlias, gladioli, hyacinths, irises, lilies and freesias. In the case of tulips, however, viruses are sometimes intentionally provoked, because they can cause the tulip's flower to change color, which is one way that new varieties are created (e.g., Rembrandt tulips).

- To control: Viruses can be transmitted from one plant to another by aphids and other sap-sucking insects. Therefore, it is necessary to keep these disease carriers in check by using the methods previously described.

OTHER PROBLEMS

Chlorosis. The leaves of plants with chlorosis turn yellow, gradually dry out (starting at the edges) and eventually drop. This phenomenon is caused by chlorophyll deficiency and generally occurs when there is a lack of iron in the soil.

- To control: Iron salts must be mixed either directly into the soil or into a mulch and then spread around the plant.

Cold damage can occur when plants are overexposed to cold weather. This usually happens either in early spring or late fall, when there is a late or early frost. Symptoms include browning of the buds and the appearance of spots on the leaves.

- To control: In areas that are prone to this kind of unpredictable weather, be sure to choose hardy species when planning your garden, especially for the summer blooming bulbs.

Etiolation is a phenomenon that manifests itself in plants grown indoors where light conditions are insufficient. Symptoms include whitening of the tissues accompanied by an abnormal elongation of the internodes.

• To control: This condition can obviously be prevented by positioning indoor plants so that they are given the correct amount of sunlight exposure.

Not all bulbs are equally sensitive to the cold. Grape hyacinths, for example, are relatively cold resistant or even very hardy, depending on the species.

SPRING BULBS

Allium
ORNAMENTAL ONION

Allium aflatunense
Family: *Liliaceae*
Height: 80 cm (31 in)

Allium aflatunense, originally from central Asia, is generally 70–100 cm (28–39 in) tall. Its compact, globe-shaped umbels are 10 cm (4 in) in diameter and comprised of tiny pinkish purple, star-shaped flowers. This hardy ornamental onion blooms in late spring (May–June) and is well suited to both fresh and dried flower bouquets. Its bulbs are planted 20 cm (8 in) deep and 25 cm (10 in) apart.

Allium is one of the best known genera of bulbous plants because many of the bulbs in this genus are essential cooking ingredients (e.g., onions, leeks, shallots and garlic). These same alimentary species also have beautiful flowers and are often used ornamentally as well. Chives (Allium schoenoprasum), for example, are commonly found both in flower and kitchen gardens. However, many of the more specifically ornamental species of

Allium (the so-called "ornamental onions") are grown solely for their aesthetic qualities. The most beautiful species are illustrated in the following pages and grouped by blooming season, earliest to latest.

Allium christophii ◄
Family: *Liliaceae*
Height: 50 cm (20 in)

Allium christophii is an ornamental onion of medium size that blooms in late spring and early summer. Although it does not always reach a full 50 cm (20 in) in height, it produces large, spherical umbels (15–20 cm [6–8 in] in diameter) consisting of approximately 50 small, metallic purple, star-shaped flowers. A dozen *Allium christophii* planted asymmetrically with pink roses and surrounded by green foliage is a winning combination for a rustic looking country garden.

Allium giganteum ►
Family: *Liliaceae*
Height: 170 cm (67 in)

Allium giganteum, originally from the Himalayan region, usually reaches 150–200 cm (59–79 in) in height, making it the tallest *Allium* species. This ornamental onion needs full sun, but is otherwise easy to grow—even in poor soil—as long as it is given proper drainage, watered during dry seasons and fertilized each fall. Its bulbs are also planted in the fall and should naturalize easily.

Allium

Allium ▶ 'Globemaster'

Family: *Liliaceae*
Height: 100 cm (39 in)

'Globemaster' is one of the most beautiful Dutch hybrids and, after *A. giganteum*, it is also one of the tallest. The many small, star-shaped flowers that make up its almost perfectly spherical umbels are more individually visible than in other varieties, making 'Globemaster' similar to the drumstick allium (*A. sphaerocephalon*). Its large purple blooms will perk up the less noticeable borders of any garden.

Allium ◀ karataviense

Family: *Liliaceae*
Height: 20 cm (8 in)

Allium karataviense, originally from the rocky regions of central Asia, grows best in warm climates, when provided with full sun, a sheltered location and free draining soil. Its umbels are composed of many small, star-shaped, white to light pink flowers and, like other small alliums, *A. karataviense* grows well in containers. Its bulbs are planted 15 cm (6 in) deep and approximately 20 cm (8 in) apart.

Allium moly ◄
Family: *Liliaceae*
Height: 30 cm (12 in)

Allium moly is a highly valued species from the northwest Mediterranean region. Its glaucous, lanceolate leaves are usually 2–3 cm (¾–1 in) wide and 15–20 cm (6–8 in) long, and wrap around the base of its bare, cylindrical stems. Unlike most ornamental onions, its inflorescence (5–8 cm [2–3 in] in diameter) is umbrella-shaped, rather than spherical, and composed of many star-shaped, uncommonly yellow florets. Its bulbs have white tunics.

Allium ◄ neapolitanum
Family: *Liliaceae*
Height: 30 cm (12 in)

As its Latin name suggests, *Allium neapolitanum* (or Naples onion) is native to the Mediterranean region. This ornamental onion grows to a height of 20–40 cm (8–16 in) and has long, keeled, ribbon-like leaves. Its umbels are generally 2 cm [¾ in] in diameter and are not as densely packed as many of the other ornamental onions. Its fragrant, milky white blooms make excellent cut flowers.

Allium

However, *A. neapolitanum* is one of the most delicate *Allium* species and must, therefore, be grown in containers and moved indoors during the colder seasons. Its natural blooming period is from April to May, but indoors it can be made to bloom earlier. It can also be propagated by separating its newly formed bulbs (or "bulbils") at the end of the growth season.

Allium nigrum ▶

Family: *Liliaceae*
Height: 70 cm (28 in)

Allium nigrum, native to the vast region that stretches from southern Europe to Iran, can commonly be found growing in grassy fields and among limestone rocks, to elevations of 2,000 m (6,560 ft). Its stems grow to a length of almost 1 m (3¼ ft). Each umbel reaches an approximate width of 8–10 cm (3–4 in) and is composed of many tiny, white flowers. There are also darker pink, red and purple varieties, which is why this species has been given the Latin name *nigrum*.

◀ Allium oreophilum

Family: *Liliaceae*
Height: 20 cm (8 in)

Originally from the Caucasus Mountain region of central Asia, *Allium oreophilum*, along with *A. karataviense*, is one of the smallest ornamental onions described in this survey. However, despite its size, it is still very popular with gardeners, not only for its delicate perfume and reddish-pink flowers, but also because it grows well in containers. Its bulbs are planted 7–8 cm (2¾–3 in) apart and 10 cm (4 in) deep and bloom from May to June. *A. oreophilum* also makes an excellent cut flower.

and sparse woodlands. From May to June it exhibits clusters of small pink and white flowers that are less numerous and compact than many of the other varieties. It has long, ribbonlike leaves and its bulbs have hard but delicate tunics.

Allium schubertii ▶
Family: *Liliaceae*
Height: 40 cm (16 in)

Allium schubertii is the strangest of all ornamental onions. Not only are its large, globelike umbels comprised of both male and female flowers, but what is particularly unique about this species is that the stems of the female flowers grow to a length of 4–5 cm (1½–2 in), while the stems of the male flowers grow to 15–20 cm (6–8 in). This odd arrangement makes the umbel look as though it is composed of two concentric spheres: the compact, inner

Allium ▲ 'Purple Sensation'
Family: *Liliaceae*
Height: 80 cm (31 in)

This beautiful *Allium aflatunense* cultivar, first registered in 1963, is similar to the original species in height (80–90 cm [31–35 in]), blooming season (May–June) and hardiness. However, 'Purple Sensation' has 10-cm (4-in) wide, spherical umbels with dark purple flowers. It is a long-lasting cut flower, and an excellent dried flower as well.

Allium roseum ▼
Family: *Liliaceae*
Height: 40 cm (16 in)

Allium roseum is a medium-sized ornamental onion, native to the Mediterranean region (Spain, Italy, Turkey and North Africa), where it can be found growing in dry, rocky soil

North Africa. The Greek etymology of its Latin name (meaning "round head") is echoed in the shape of its bloom. Its ball-shaped blooms also inspired its common name, drumstick allium. Although each individual flower is extremely tiny, together they form a compact purple ball with white specks. Each umbel is supported by a 60–70 cm (24–28 in) stem surrounded by long, thin leaves. Its leaves are the same length as its stems, but droop towards the ground before the plant has bloomed. Drumstick allium combines beautifully with fountain grass (*Pennisetum alopecuroides*), gray-leafed artemisia and some species of hosta.

63

sphere holds the female flowers, while the more sparsely occupied outer sphere holds the male flowers. *A. schubertii* is native to Israel and Syria and should be protected from the cold or grown in containers in cooler regions. Its 30-cm (12-in) wide umbels make dazzling cut or dried flowers.

Allium ▶
sphaerocephalon
Family: *Liliaceae*
Height: 60 cm (24 in)

Allium sphaerocephalon is native to the meadows and drier regions of Europe and

Allium

While most bulbous plants belong to the Iridaceae, Liliaceae *or* Amaryllidaceae *families, there are many bulbous representatives from other families as well. Anemones, for example, are bulbous plants belonging to the* Ranunculaceae *family, which also includes the* Eranthis *and* Ranunculus *genera. Anemones bloom in both spring and summer, depending on the variety.* Anemone blanda *and its hybrids are spring bloomers, while* Anemone coronaria *and its hybrids are summer bloomers.*

Anemone blanda ▲ 'Blue Shades'

Family: *Ranunculaceae*
Height: 15 cm (6 in)

The differences between the many varieties of *Anemone blanda* (windflowers) are rather minute. Windflowers are generally very hardy and adapt easily to new environments. 'Blue Shades' is a small perennial that grows to a height of less than 20 cm (8 in), and in March and April produces small flowers with long violet petals; the 'Atro-caerulea' variety has dark blue flowers. Its tuberous rhizomes are planted 5 cm (2 in) deep and 5 cm (2 in) apart and are ideal container plants because they do not require much growing space. Its leaves are triangular and divided into three sections.

Anemone blanda ▶ 'White Splendor'

Family: Ranunculaceae
Height: 15 cm (6 in)

The only real difference between this particular variety and other *A. blanda* is its lovely white flower. Although windflowers are often sold as mixed colors, enthusiasts tend to pick a color and stick with it. Low-lying, monochromatic clusters of white, pink, purple or blue are lovely when planted against a contrasting background of taller flowers.

Anemone blanda ◀ 'Pink Star'

Family: *Ranunculaceae*
Height: 15 cm (6 in)

'Pink Star' has bright magenta flowers with white inner rings, but otherwise is very similar to the other *Anemone blanda* presented in this section. They grow well in both full and partial sun and alkaline and acidic soil, as long as they have sufficient drainage. Their rhizomes can stay in the ground year-round. Always take special care to cut their flowers with a knife or a pair of scissors: pulling at their stems can cause damage to the root structure.

Brimeura amethystina 'Alba'
Family: *Liliaceae*
Height: 20 cm (8 in)

While its Latin name refers to its typically amethyst-colored flowers, there are also white, pale blue, dark blue and violet varieties. 'Alba,' for example, is a pure white variety that grows to a height of 20–25 cm (8–10 in) and, in the spring, produces numerous bell-shaped flowers, generally 2.5–5 cm (1–2 in) in diameter. Its bright green leaves are grooved and linear.

Its blooming season begins in April, but reaches its peak in May and can sometimes last through June. Its bulbs are planted 10 cm (4 in) deep and 7–8 cm (2½–3 in) apart.

Brimeura amethystina, also called the amethyst hyacinth, is native to the Pyrenean region, but is also common in Spain and the northwestern Balkans. Amethyst hyacinths grow well in mountain meadows and dry, calcareous soil, in both full and partial sun, depending on species and geographic location.

Brimeura *are small, charming plants, aesthetically similar to bellflowers* (Campanulaceae) *and are generally 10–25 cm (4–10 in) tall. For best results, plant a good number of bulbs so that they are not visually overpowered by larger flowers.* Brimeura *work well in rock gardens and borders.*

Camassia

Camassia is a hardy North American species that requires moist soil and is very sensitive to summer drought. In September, Camassia (or camas) rapidly produces many bulbils that can soon be detached from the mother bulb. New plants can also be grown from seed, but will only begin flowering after four to five years.

Camassia cusickii ▼
Family: *Liliaceae*
Height: 70 cm (28 in)

While generally reaching an average height of 70 cm (28 in), some individuals have been known to exceed 100 cm (39 in). The basal leaves of *Camassia cusickii* (also called cusick camas) are slender, linear and sage-colored. Its stems terminate in pointed racemes composed of many small, slightly pink-tinted, blue flowers. Each flower is generally 2.5–5 cm (1–2 in) wide. Its bulbs are planted 15 cm (6 in) deep and 20 cm (8 in) apart.

▲
Camassia leichtlinii 'Caerulea'
Family: *Liliaceae*
Height: 80 cm (31 in)

Camassia leichtlinii (or great camas), while very similar to *C. cusickii,* is usually taller (reaching a maximum height of 140 cm [55 in]) and has much larger flowers (7–8 cm [2½– 3 in] in diameter). The many varieties of *C. leichtlinii* (e.g., 'Caerulea,' 'Alba' and 'Atro-caerulea') have white, pink, turquoise, cerulean or violet blooms. *C. leichtlinii* are suitable for borders or beds and create wonderful accents when planted in dense clusters.

Chionodoxa
Glory-of-the-Snow

As its common name alludes, glory-of-the-snow blooms from late winter to early spring, often when there is still snow on the ground. The Chionodoxa *genus is native to Asia Minor.*

Chionodoxa ▶ forbesii
Family: *Liliaceae*
Height: 15 cm (6 in)

Chionodoxa forbesii is a small bulbous plant that does not exceed 20 cm (8 in) in height. It has two basal leaves with blunted ends and a short stem, supporting a raceme of a few star-shaped, white flowers. Each individual flower has six tepals attached at the base of a short tube, which contains the yellow-tipped filaments. Its bulbs are planted in the fall, 10 cm (4 in) deep (or less) and the same distance apart, in full or partial sun.

The pink glory-of-the-snow (shown in the photo) is a popular variety.

Chionodoxa ▼ luciliae
Family: *Liliaceae*
Height: 15 cm (6 in)

Chionodoxa luciliae has the same physical characteristics and planting requirements as *C. forbesii*, but the popular 'Alba' variety has delicate white flowers with yellow centers. Glory-of-the-snow is at home in all types of gardens, but is particularly well suited to rock gardens. It is also easily naturalized and can stay in the ground year-round with little difficulty.

Chionodoxa

Corydalis

Corydalis solida
Family: *Papaveraceae*
Height: 15 cm (6 in)

Corydalis solida is a small plant with straight, glabrous stems reaching a maximum height of 15–20 cm (6–8 in). Its lower leaves are mere scales, while its upper leaves are glaucous, deeply cleft and vaguely fernlike. From March to May *C. solida* produces clusters of tubular, lavender flowers with darker violet mouths. Other varieties of *Corydalis* range from white to dark purple. While *Corydalis* are generally not used as cut flowers and do not make good houseplants, they do grow well in large patio containers as long as they are provided with free draining soil. The bulbs are small and yellowish.

69

Among the many bulbs described in this survey, Corydalis is the only member of the poppy family that has been included. The Corydalis genus is native to Europe with a vast range that extends from France to the Ukraine, and from Norway to Turkey. It prefers shady, out-of-the-way corners of the garden, next to a low wall or nestled between large rocks. Its bulbs are planted in the fall, 5 cm (2 in) deep and 7–8 cm (2½–3 in) apart. It does not require watering or fertilizer and does well in poor, moist soil. Corydalis can be propagated by seed or bulb division at the end of the growing season. Corydalis solida (or Corydalis bulbosa), C. cashmiriana and C. lutea are all members of the genus.

Crocus

The crocus is native to Asia Minor and the Mediterranean coastal region. The popularity of this little flower dates back to ancient Greece and Rome, where it was commonly planted around gravesites, because it was believed that the flower brought luck to the soul as it passed into the afterlife.

Today, the many varieties of crocus are still extremely popular and their yellow, white or purple flowers are among the first signs of spring. Their small size also makes them particularly well suited to window boxes, which become lovely carpets of color as soon as the temperature starts to rise. There are even some varieties of crocus (snow crocuses) that bloom when the ground is still covered with snow. Their upward-facing, bell-shaped flowers grow low to the ground and are surrounded by taller, emerald green, grasslike leaves, with a silver stripe running down the middle.

Crocus 'Ard Schenk'

Family: *Iridaceae*
Height: 10 cm (4 in)

'Ard Schenk,' like all crocuses, does not grow very tall, but this splendid winter–spring variety produces beautiful white blooms in February and March. Its small corms are planted approximately 10 cm (4 in) deep and 8 cm (3 in) apart in early fall.

Crocus ◄ 'Cream Beauty'
Family: *Iridaceae*
Height: 10 cm (4 in)

Although 'Cream Beauty' is one of the smaller varieties—not always reaching a full 10 cm (4 in) in height—it is still much sought after for its fragrant perfume, a rarity for this genus. 'Cream Beauty,' derived from the white-petaled species (*Crocus chrysanthus*), has creamy yellow flowers with golden throats and light, fan-shaped stripes on the outer side of its petals.

Crocus ► 'Flower Record'
Family: *Iridaceae*
Height: 10 cm (4 in)

'Flower Record' has unevenly colored violet flowers that are darker at the tips. Its linear leaves are dark green with white central veins. 'Flower Record' is one of many Dutch crocuses derived from the species *Crocus vernus*. 'Flower Record' is also strikingly similar to the saffron crocus (*Crocus sativus*), from which the expensive kitchen spice is extracted.

Crocus ◄ 'Fuscotinctus'
Family: *Iridaceae*
Height: 10 cm (4 in)

'Fuscotinctus' is similar in appearance to 'Cream Beauty,' but with brighter yellow flowers, darker stripes and no perfume. Its corm, like most crocuses, is 2 cm (¾ in) in diameter and almost spherical—slightly flattened at the poles. Its outer scales are thin, filamentous and dark copper in color.

Crocus ► 'Golden Bunch'
Family: *Iridaceae*
Height: 10 cm (4 in)

'Golden Bunch' is almost identical to the other crocuses described in this section, except for its uniform, golden yellow flowers. In February and March, each plant produces many tiny flowers in rapid succession. Crocuses do not require any particular soil preparation, but should not be planted more than 10 cm (4 in) deep.

Crocus ◄ 'Grand Maître'
Family: *Iridaceae*
Height: 10 cm (4 in)

'Grand Maître,' another *Crocus vernus* variety, is notable for its purple flowers with bright orange centers. Less precocious than some of the other varieties, its flowers do not appear until March, but last for the entire month. The white and purple crocuses come in a range of different color combinations; for example, pale or dark blue with cobalt edges. The yellow crocuses also range in color, from lemon yellow with gold nuances to bronze.

Crocus ► 'Jeanne d'Arc'
Family: *Iridaceae*
Height: 10 cm (4 in)

This unique variety of *Crocus vernus* has snow white blooms with subtle orange pistils. Their small size and early blooming period make them perfect for growing in large containers, where they can be planted together with other bulbs. Crocuses, arranged around the container's outer edge, will be the first to bloom and when their flowers have withered, the small, dark green leaves that remain make a nice border for daffodils or tulips.

Crocus

Crocus ◄ 'Moonlight'

Family: *Iridaceae*
Height: 10 cm (4 in)

'Moonlight,' popular for its muted yellow flowers and early blooming period, pairs nicely with violets, particularly *Viola odorata,* which has small lavender or dark violet blooms. Both crocuses and violets should be planted in the fall and can be left in the ground year-round.

Crocus 'Pickwick' ►

Family: *Iridaceae*
Height: 15 cm (6 in)

Although 'Pickwick' reaches a maximum height of only 12–15 cm (5–6 in), it is still one of tallest crocuses. Its flowers have thin, irregular, purple and white stripes, and the inner sides of its petal are slightly darker than the outer sides. For best results, plant corms in the fall—earlier or later depending on local climate.

Crocus ▼
'Ruby Giant'
Family: *Iridaceae*
Height: 10 cm (4 in)

'Ruby Giant,' a variety of *Crocus tommasinianus,* is native to the Balkan coastal regions. Like most crocuses, it grows happily in full sun, in rock gardens, at the base of a deciduous tree and in borders of herbaceous perennials. Its bright lavender-pink flowers have made it a garden favorite.

Crocuses are nice when planted in the lawn because their dark green, grasslike

Crocus ▲
'Prins Claus'
Family: *Iridaceae*
Height: 10 cm (4 in)

Although many crocuses have white and purple flowers, 'Prins Claus' is unique for the elegant way in which these two colors are combined. Each white flower is interrupted by only a brush stroke of dark purple, fading to white, on the outer side of each petal and by bright red and yellow pistils.

Although crocuses come in many wonderful colors, they do not make good cut flowers

because they wilt very quickly after they have been cut. Crocuses can still be enjoyed indoors, however, because they grow beautifully in containers. Simply place your planted container of crocuses outside during the winter and when the flowers begin to bud, bring them indoors and watch them bloom.

leaves make the lawn appear more lush, even after the flowers have withered. However, avoid mowing the lawn until the crocus leaves have also withered; without their leaves they can not accumulate and store the energy needed to survive the winter and produce next year's blooms.

Crocus ▲ 'Whitewell Purple'
Family: Iridaceae
Height: 10 cm (4 in)

'Whitewell Purple' is another variety of *Crocus tommasinianus,* named after the 18th century Italian botanist, Muzio Tommasini. While similar in appearance to 'Ruby Giant,' the flowers of 'Whitewell Purple' are a more reddish violet color with silvery white reflections on the inside of each petal. Like all crocuses, 'Whitewell Purple' is easy to grow, but best results are obtained when planted in large groups. Mixed color assortments of light, dark or bicolor varieties, often with visible contrasting veins, are also very popular both indoors and out. Two or three flowers often grow from one bulb, with the number of flowers increasing after the first year.

Cyclamen

Cyclamen coum
Family: *Primulaceae*
Height: 10 cm (4 in)

Cyclamen coum is native to the vast region surrounding the Black Sea, extending from Bulgaria to the Caucasus Mountains, to Turkey and as far south as Lebanon. It is a small plant, usually not more than 7–8 cm (2½–3 in) tall, with flat, heart-shaped leaves that range from dark green to dark red, but most commonly are mosaics of light and dark green patterns. It is best known, however, for its brightly colored flowers which, depending on variety and location, can be scarlet, pink or white. Some varieties even have white flowers with purple specks.

Cyclamens can only be propagated by seed, which if planted in the fall, germinate the following spring. Tubers, unlike other types of bulbs, cannot be divided; they simply get bigger and produce more flowers. Given the proper conditions, however, a cyclamen will continue to grow for decades.

Among the many flowering bulbs, there is no lack of representatives from the Primulaceae family, including the popular cyclamen, which is often sold as a houseplant. Cyclamens are unique because their primary blooming season is fall–winter, although there are a few species that bloom in spring and summer. Cyclamen persicum is among the most common species of the winter–spring blooming cyclamens and its bulbs are primarily used for forcing indoors. Cyclamen coum is another hardy species that begins blooming in early spring through the end of May. Cyclamens grow well in shady locations, in light, permeable soil that is high in organic matter.

Eranthis

9

Eranthis, *native to south central Europe, it is one of the few flowering bulbs found in the* Ranunculaceae *family.* Eranthis hyemalis, *or winter aconite, blooms in late winter (February–March). Winter aconites do not have particular climatic requirements and adapt well to all types of soil, as long as it is not too dry. Once the plants have become acclimatized to their new surroundings, they will begin to propagate spontaneously by seed, forming lovely compact colonies.*

Eranthis hyemalis
Family: *Ranunculaceae*
Height: 10 cm (4 in)

The winter aconite is a low-growing species that produces attractive yellow, cuplike flowers that seem to sit on little green saucers made of sessile leaves that widen towards the flower's base. Its rhizomes are planted in the fall, 10 cm (4 in) deep and 6–8 cm (2–3 in) apart.

Eremurus
DESERT CANDLE (OR FOXTAIL LILY)

10

The Eremurus *genus is native to much of central Asia, from Turkey to the foothills of the Himalayas, where it grows primarily on dry and rocky hillsides or in pastures with heavy soil. These spectacular plants have large, fleshy, star-shaped roots, and can sometimes grow to a height of 3 m (10 ft). Their long, thin leaves are usually left alone by herbivores.*

Eremurus stenophyllus
Family: *Liliaceae*
Height: 100 cm (39 in)

Eremurus stenophyllus is a very tall species that commonly reaches a height of 1 m (3¼ ft) or more. It blooms from mid-June through July and prefers sandy soil, or soil where sand has been added. Its rhizomes need to be planted only 10 cm (4 in) deep, but should be spaced at least 50 cm (20 in) apart. It makes an excellent cut flower.

flower's bulb is only about 2 cm (¾ in) wide. Common to all species, however, are their pendant, bell-shaped flowers. Ironically the smallest species have the largest flowers. The largest fritillary flowers are 4 cm (1½ in) in diameter. The crown imperial commonly grows to 1 m (3¼ ft) in height, while the guinea hen flower rarely exceeds 20 cm (8 in).

Fritillaria imperialis 'Maxima Lutea'

Family: *Liliaceae*
Height: 80 cm (31 in)

This impressive crown imperial often reaches a height of 1 m (3¼ ft). Its tall, stalklike stems send up a tuft of spiky leaves perched atop a crown of nodding yellow flowers that bloom in April and May. 'Maxima Lutea' requires a temperate climate (it does not like the cold), full sun and free-draining, fertile soil. Its bulbs should be planted 30 cm (12 in) apart and a good 20 cm (8 in) deep, surrounded by a layer of sand. They should also be placed on a slightly tilted axis in the ground to keep stagnant water from accumulating on the large bulbs. Fertilize every year with well-rotted manure and water regularly.

The different Fritillaria *species have very diverse origins. The guinea hen flower (*Fritillaria meleagris*), for example, is native to central Europe, while the crown imperial (*Fritillaria imperialis*) has Iranian, Afghani and Kashmiri origins; there are even some North American species.*

All fritillaries, however, prefer regions where the winters are snowy and the summers are hot and dry. Fritillary bulbs are also quite different from one another, especially in size. The bulb of the crown imperial, for example, is about the size of a fist, while the guinea hen

Fritillaria

81

Fritillaria imperialis 'Rubra Maxima'

Family: *Liliaceae*
Height: 80 cm (31 in)

The crown imperial is so called because its cluster of brightly colored bell-shaped flowers sit like a crown atop tall bare stems. The flowers of the crown imperial can be golden yellow, orange or red like those of 'Rubra Maxima.' Crown imperials also make long-lasting cut flowers and are the perfect centerpiece for any floral arrangement. For an impressive display of color, plant different colors in clusters of 10 in the farthest corner of the garden along a wall or a fence.

Fritillaria

82

Fritillaria ▼ michailovskyi

Family: *Liliaceae*
Height: 20 cm (8 in)

There are approximately 100 species in the *Fritillaria* genus, but only a few are commonly cultivated. *Fritillaria michailovskyi,* one of the more common species, rarely exceeds 20 cm (8 in) in height and, like other fritillaries, blooms in April and May.

Fritillaria ▲ meleagris

Family: *Liliaceae*
Height: 25 cm (10 in)

Fritillaria meleagris is also galled the guinea hen flower because its flowers resemble the checkered feathers of a guinea hen. This species is one of the smaller fritillaries,

reaching a maximum height of 20–25 cm (8–10 in), or 40–45 cm (16–18 in) for certain varieties. Guinea hen flowers come in many different colors, are easily naturalized and give your garden a wonderful bucolic accent when combined with other naturalizing species.

Its small size makes it perfect for growing in pots and window boxes. Its bulbs are planted 10–15 cm (4–6 in) deep and 15 cm (6 in) apart.

Fritillaria persica ▲
Family: *Liliaceae*
Height: 80 cm (31 in)

The Persian fritillary (*Fritillaria persica*) is similar in size to the crown imperial and has similar planting requirements. Fritillary bulbs are delicate and must be handled with care. A healthy bulb should be unbroken and firm to the touch. They also have a naturally pungent odor, which is not the sign of an unhealthy bulb. Fritillaries can be propagated by bulbils or seeds.

Galanthus
SNOWDROP

Like cyclamens, snowdrops are winter–spring bulbs that bloom from January–February to March–April. The many species that make up this genus have white flowers with three outer tepals, and three smaller, inner tepals with green markings at the tips. They also have long ribbonlike leaves with blunted ends.

Galanthus nivalis ▶
Family: *Amaryllidaceae*
Height: 10 cm (4 in)

This species grows naturally in cold, damp woodlands, but even its cultivars, while hardy and easy to grow, prefer moist, fertile, well-drained soil and partial shade. Its bulbs are planted in fall, 5–10 cm (2–4 in) deep and approximately 10 cm (4 in) apart.

Galanthus nivalis 'Flore Plenum' ▶
Family: *Amaryllidaceae*
Height: 10 cm (4 in)

This *Galanthus nivalis* cultivar has maintained many of the original characteristics of the botanical species; the main variation is that 'Flore Plenum' has a double flower. Other snowdrop cultivars, on the other hand, have been bred to bloom later in the spring.

84

Galanthus

Geranium

Although the Geraniaceae *family is not one of the three classic bulb families (*Liliaceae, Iridaceae *and* Amaryllidaceae*), no bulb survey would be complete without it. These geraniums, however, should not be confused with those of the* Pelargonium *genus.* Pelargoniums *are commonly called geraniums, while the members of the* Geranium *genus are generally referred to as "true geraniums" or "hardy geraniums."* Geranium transversale *is a tuberous geranium native to north central Asia, including some portions of Siberia. It blooms in open fields and low-lying hills in April and May, as does the Mediterranean species,* Geranium tuberosum*, which can be found growing naturally all over Europe.*

Geranium tuberosum

Family: *Geraniaceae*
Height: 20 cm (8 in)

This species of geranium has thin, bare stems and tiny purple flowers with dark purple veins, only 8–12 mm (¼–½ in) in diameter. Its basal leaves are sage-colored and have segmented lamina (divided into five to seven segments) comprised of numerous linear lacinia. *Geranium tuberosum* is easy to grow, but prefers a dry, sunny location, in free-draining soil. Its large tuberous roots with one to three ovoid tubercles are planted in the spring, and can stay in the ground year-round. *G. tuberosum* blooms in March or April through the end of May. It can be propagated by seed, shoot cuttings or dividing its tuberous roots in early spring. Its tuberous roots are planted 5–10 cm (2–4 in) deep and 10–20 cm (4–8 in) apart.

Hippeastrum ◀ 'Aphrodite'
Family: *Amaryllidaceae*
Height: 55 cm (22 in)

This hybrid's white petals, outlined in red, combine the two colors of this genus in a new and delicately elegant way.

Hippeastrum ▼ 'Apple Blossom'
Family: *Amaryllidaceae*
Height: 55 cm (22 in)

Although the flowers of 'Apple Blossom' are the same colors as 'Aphrodite,' they differ considerably in appearance because of the way in which the two colors are

87

Like the "geraniums" of the Perigonium *genus, the "amaryllis" of the* Hippeastrum *genus are not true amaryllises. The name "amaryllis" rightfully belongs to* Amaryllis bel-ladonna, *the single species in the* Amaryllis *genus. While* A. belladonna *is very similar in appearance to the* Hippeastrum *species, the two genera are actually very different. The delicate, South American* Hippeas-trum *are winter–spring bloomers and can generally be cultivated only indoors, while the fall–winter bloom-ing* A. belladonna *is much*

hardier and can easily be grown in the garden. Although there are many naturally occurring species of Hippeastrum, *only hybrids are readily avail-able. The hybrids are almost identical to one another except for the color of their blooms.*

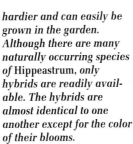

combined. The petals of 'Apple Blossom' also have a heavier consistency, making them appear less delicate.

Hippeastrum ▾ 'Green Goddess'
Family: *Amaryllidaceae*
Height: 55 cm (22 in)

'Green Goddess' is an unusual member of this genus because its flowers are almost pure white with lime-green throats and no trace of the characteristic red or pink tones. *Hippeastrum* are extremely cold sensitive and can be planted outdoors only in very warm climates, in partial shade and moist, rich soil. In most climates these luscious beauties must be grown indoors and bloom in winter and spring.

Hippeastrum ▴ 'Double Record'
Family: *Amaryllidaceae*
Height: 55 cm (22 in)

Another delightful variation on the standard red and white color combination is found in this hybrid's remarkable double blooms. 'Double Record' is otherwise almost identical to the other *Hippeastrum* hybrids. It has a large bulb with a diameter of 8–10 cm (3–4 in), and each 45–70 cm (18–28 in) stem is topped with two to five (usually three) large, trumpet-shaped flowers, usually 15 cm (6 in) in diameter.

Hippeastrum ▶ 'Hercules'

Family: *Amaryllidaceae*
Height: 55 cm (22 in)

In contrast to the nearly pure white 'Green Goddess,' the 'Hercules' cultivar is totally red. Like all *Hippeastrum*, it has light green leaves that fan away from the stem.

Hippeastrum ▼ 'Jewel'

Family: *Amaryllidaceae*
Height: 55 cm (22 in)

'Jewel,' like the other hybrids, can be potted indoors in the spring (or in the fall for winter blooms), taking care to leave the tip of the bulb poking out of the soil. Plant only

Hippeastrum ▼ 'Lady Jane'

Family: *Amaryllidaceae*
Height: 55 cm (22 in)

The unique red and white, peppermint-striped blossoms of 'Lady Jane' make beautiful cut flowers. Once potted, these bulbs require little water, but watering should be increased when the first flowers and leaves begin to appear.

one bulb per container, in light, fertile soil that is equal parts potting soil, peat and sand.

Hippeastrum ▶ 'Las Vegas'

Family: *Amaryllidaceae*
Height: 55 cm (22 in)

'Las Vegas' offers spectacular large, red blooms with wide white stripes running down the center of each petal. In climates that permit outdoor planting, bulbs should be protected with a heavy layer of mulch or plastic tarp during the winter to protect them from excessive moisture.

Hippeastrum ◀ 'Lemon Lime'

Family: *Amaryllidaceae*
Height: 55 cm (22 in)

'Lemon Lime' produces delicate lemon white blooms with green throats that are the same green color as its leaves. When planting indoors, the container should not be much larger than the bulb itself and does not necessarily need to have drainage holes at the bottom.

Hippeastrum ▶ 'Minerva'

Family: *Amaryllidaceae*
Height: 55 cm (22 in)

The varieties of *Hippeastrum* increase each year as new hybrids with new color combinations are created. 'Minerva'

Hippeastrum

has distinct red-tipped flowers with pure white centers and red veins that radiate towards the petals' outer edges like a ball of fire.

Hippeastrum ▶ 'Mont Blanc'
Family: *Amaryllidaceae*
Height: 55 cm (22 in)

All *Hippeastrum* have trumpet-shaped flowers with six starlike petals that are more or less pointed at the tips. The colors red and white are also ever present, but each hybrid is unique, thanks to the varying shades of red and pink (including red, white, pink, salmon, crimson, etc.) and the endless patterns (stripes, borders, spots, etc.) found in each variety. The entirely red bloom is at one end of the color spectrum, while the entirely white bloom is at the other. The snow white petals of 'Mont Blanc' are interrupted only by its light green throat.

Hippeastrum ▼ 'Orange Sovereign'
Family: *Amaryllidaceae*
Height: 55 cm (22 in)

This hybrid's intense orange-red blooms with dark red venation are highly valued and usually bloom eight to 10 weeks after planting. This process can be accelerated, however, by placing the container in a warm sunny spot and watering daily. Likewise, flowering can be delayed by placing it in a dark cool spot and watering less frequently.

To obtain a series of consecutive blooms, plant one bulb every 10 to 15 days from October to January.

Hippeastrum ◄ 'Piquant'
Family: *Amaryllidaceae*
Height: 55 cm (22 in)

'Piquant' looks like a cross between 'Lady Jane' and 'Minerva.' When its flowers begin to wither, cut its stems and move it to a cooler, but still sunny location and continue to water and fertilize until the leaves have completely withered.

Hippeastrum ▼ 'Red Lion'
Family: *Amaryllidaceae*
Height: 55 cm (22 in)

The particularly stunning, vibrant red blooms with bright yellow anthers of 'Red Lion' make great centerpiece flowers in mixed bouquets. Its bulbs are usually sold individually and should be firm, compact and relatively weighty. Roots should also be present, but are rather delicate, so be careful not to damage or break them while planting.

Hippeastrum ◄ 'Red Peacock'
Family: *Amaryllidaceae*
Height: 55 cm (22 in)

'Red Peacock' should be planted in snug-fitting containers: do not cover the tops of the bulbs with soil.

Hippeastrum ► 'Vera'

Family: *Amaryllidaceae*
Height: 55 cm (22 in)

The flowers of 'Vera' are the same color and shape as the spring–summer blooming *Amaryllis*. The summer growing season ends six weeks after the flowers have wilted, when the leaves have also dried up. At this point, the stem should be cut at 5 cm (2 in) above the top of the bulb with a sharp knife and all irrigation and fertilization should be stopped. When the soil has dried completely, move to a cold, dark area where the bulb can be stored until the following season.

Hippeastrum ► 'Voodoo'

Family: *Amaryllidaceae*
Height: 55 cm (22 in)

'Voodoo' produces brilliant red blooms with white centers and dark green throats. As for all *Hippeastrum,* if the flower appears to be unstable, tie it to a small support stick but be careful not to spear the roots when inserting the support.

Hyacinthoides
BLUEBELL

15

94

Hyacinthoides hispanica 'Excelsior'
Family: *Liliaceae*
Height: 30 cm (12 in)

Hyacinthoides hispanica, or "Spanish bluebells," are native to the western Mediterranean region, including Spain, Morocco and Algeria. Spanish bluebells have spherical bulbs, long, bending, linear leaves and sturdy, stalklike stems, terminating in clusters of five to 15 small lavender campanulate flowers. While the flowers of the *H. hispanica* species are almost completely odorless, the 'Excelsior' variety has a delicate perfume. Spanish bluebells thrive in moist soil that is high in organic matter, in rock gardens and in the partial shade of deciduous trees or other tall plants. The bulbs are planted 10 cm (4 in) deep and the same distance apart and can be left in the soil year-round. The fragile bulbs, lacking a protective outer tunic, should also be transplanted as little as possible. The species naturalizes and spreads easily, and can be propagated by bulbils or seeds.

Many of the species found in the large and crowded Liliaceae *family are similar and, therefore, difficult to classify.* Hyacinthoides hispanica, *for example, is sometimes placed in the* Scilla *genus as* Scilla hispanica. *It is also sometimes referred to as* Endymion hispanicus.

Hyacinthoides

Hyacinthoides 'Rose'

Family: *Liliaceae*
Height: 30 cm (12 in)

While the most common color of *Hyacinthoides,* both Spanish and English bluebells (*H. hispanica* and *H. non-scripta* or *H. nutans*), is violet-blue, there are pale blue, white and even pink varieties, like 'Rose,' shown here. 'Rose' blooms in May and has a pleasant fragrance. It makes an excellent cut flower, but is not well suited to forcing.

Hyacinthus
HYACINTH

16

Hyacinthus ◄ 'Anna Marie'
Family: *Liliaceae*
Height: 25 cm (10 in)

Almost every variety of hyacinth grows to a height of 25–30 cm (10–12 in) and 'Anna Marie' is no exception. Its bulbs have typically pointed tops, from which its leaves and flowers grow, and flat bottoms, from which the roots grow. Its bulbs are planted 15–20 cm (6–8 in) deep and 15 cm (6 in) apart.

The Middle Eastern hyacinth has been popular since the time of the Ottoman Turks, but while there are many naturally occurring species almost all of the hyacinths that grow in our gardens today are Dutch hybrids, derived from the Hyacinthus orientalis species. H. orientalis hybrids all have semisucculent, wide, linear leaves. Their waxy, sweet-smelling, funnel-shaped florets are 2–3 cm (³/₄–1 in) wide and clustered together in a 15-cm (6-in) long inflorescence supported by a thick, sturdy stem. The bulbs are planted in September or October and will grow happily in a sunny location, in light, sandy, well-drained soil. The bulbs, however, must be extracted from the soil after the leaves have yellowed, and stored for the summer in a dry, well-ventilated location. They can be planted again the in the fall, but because hyacinths tend to produce smaller florets every year, bulbs should be replaced after three or four seasons.

96

Hyacinthus

Hyacinthus ▼ 'Atlantic'

Family: *Liliaceae*
Height: 25 cm (10 in)

The 'Atlantic' variety is aptly named for the unique color of its flowers, which evoke the deep blue color of the ocean. The color of a hyacinth's flowers can be determined by examining its bulb tunic. White or yellow hyacinths have white tunics, pink or red hyacinths have reddish tunics and blue or purple hyacinths have purple tunics.

Hyacinthus ▲ 'Blue Jacket'

Family: *Liliaceae*
Height: 25 cm (10 in)

Blue hyacinths, like 'Blue Jacket,' are very popular with bulb lovers because they are among the few spring-blooming bulbs with blue flowers. However, hyacinths, planted together with tulips and daffodils, will not only reward you with their beauty, but also with their delicious scent.

Hyacinthus ▼ 'Carnegie'

Family: *Liliaceae*
Height: 25 cm (10 in)

'Carnegie,' first cultivated in the early 1900s, still enjoys tremendous popularity, thanks to its unusual white flowers that are distinctly different from the soft, cream-colored blooms of 'City of Haarlem,' or the lucent, pearl-colored flowers of 'White Pearl.' All white hyacinths, however, pair nicely with lilac pansies, while light blue hyacinths and yellow pansies make a nice display.

Hyacinthus ▲ 'Blue Star'

Family: *Liliaceae*
Height: 25 cm (10 in)

'Blue Star' is another hyacinth with deep violet blooms, and like all flowering bulbs, it grows best when good quality bulbs are used. Healthy bulbs are firm to the touch and do not have cracks, markings or mold on their surface. The papery outer tunics, however, do not need to be intact.

Hyacinthus ▶
'Delft Blue'
Family: *Liliaceae*
Height: 25 cm (10 in)

The pale blue flowers of the 'Delft Blue' cultivar (named for the Dutch city of Delft) are a softer hue than many of the more traditional blue hyacinths. The pale lilac color of their blossoms is reminiscent of traditional Dutch ceramics.

Hyacinthus ◀
'Fondant'
Family: *Liliaceae*
Height: 25 cm (10 in)

Among the many varieties of pink hyacinths, 'Fondant' has the most delicate pink blooms, and makes an impressive display when planted in a sunny corner of the garden, away from the permanent shade of trees. Its bulbs are planted late in the fall (October–November), in well-turned soil.

Hyacinthus ◄ 'Jan Bos'
Family: *Liliaceae*
Height: 25 cm (10 in)

The intense fuchsia—almost red—color of this cultivar makes 'Jan Bos' excellent for forcing, because it will light up any dark corner of your home during the dreary winter months. The easiest way to force bulbs is to buy bulbs that have already been "prepared" for this purpose; these bulbs are usually readily available.

Hyacinthus ► 'Gypsy Queen'
Family: *Liliaceae*
Height: 25 cm (10 in)

The delightfully unusual salmon pink color of 'Gypsy Queen' makes a wonderful garden accent. For a concentrated block of color, plant bulbs in clusters, approximately 15 cm (6 in) apart, or farther apart to leave room for other plants. In either case, however, bulbs should be planted in an area where the soil has been properly prepared and covered with a layer of soil equal to two times their height.

Hyacinthus ◄ 'Multiflora'
Family: *Liliaceae*
Height: 25 cm (10 in)

As its name suggests, 'Multiflora' produces multiple flower stems for every bulb. However, it is shorter than many other hyacinths and produces fewer flowers per stem. Plant the lilac, white and pink 'Multiflora' varieties together for light, colorful and natural-looking borders.

Hyacinthus ► 'Pink Pearl'
Family: *Liliaceae*
Height: 25 cm (10 in)

'Pink Pearl' has beautiful pearly rose flowers and is the perfect choice for a formal garden in square, circular or semicircular flowerbeds or in simple, thickly planted borders. For best results, plant bulbs 12–14 cm (5–5½ in) apart.

Iris

17

Iris 'Apollo' ◄
Family: *Iridaceae*
Height: 60 cm (24 in)

While the flowers of most irises are composed of two contrasting colors, 'Apollo' is popular for its uncommonly subtle blend of yellows. The flowers of 'Apollo' have light yellow standards with darker yellow falls that are darkest at the center of each petal.

Iris bucharica ◄
Family: *Iridaceae*
Height: 25 cm (10 in)

Iris bucharica is native to the grassy and rocky regions of Afghanistan and central Asia, where it grows like a radiant wildflower in the hot sun. It produces fragrant white and yellow flowers in March and April and can be anywhere from 15 to 45 cm (6–18 in) tall. Its bulbs are planted 10 cm (4 in) deep and the same distance apart in well-drained soil.

Many of the approximately 300 species found in the Iris genus are "bulbous irises." Irises are easy to recognize because of their uniquely shaped flowers, composed of two sets of three petals connected at their base. The three external petals, or "falls," droop down and away from the center of the flower, while the three internal petals, or "standards," stand upright. Irises also have three stamens located inside the falls, and a petal-like stigma.

Iris danfordiae ◄

Family: *Iridaceae*
Height: 10 cm (4 in)

Iris danfordiae is a "rock garden iris" originally from central Turkey, where it can be found growing naturally in wide, open spaces and well-drained soil at elevations of 2,000–3,000 m (6,560–9,840 ft). It produces bright yellow flowers with green-speckled throats in late winter to early spring. Despite the fact that *I. danfordiae* is generally not more than 10 cm (4 in) tall, it is still one of the most commonly cultivated botanical species, and one of the top 100 most popular irises. Its miniature size also makes it perfect for growing in containers, as in the garden it risks being overshadowed by the larger varieties.

Iris 'Casablanca' ►

Family: *Iridaceae*
Height: 60 cm (24 in)

As its name alludes, 'Casablanca' is a pure white iris with a typical, yellow, tongue-like marking at the center of each fall. It is easily identifiable as a cultivar because of its height: all cultivars in this genus reach a standard height of 60 cm (24 in). 'Casablanca' is also similar in appearance to and therefore sometimes confused with two other white irises: 'Madonna' and 'White Wedgwood.'

Iris 'Hildegarde' ◄
Family: *Iridaceae*
Height: 60 cm (24 in)

Although there are many popular botanical, or naturally occurring species of irises (e.g., *I. danfordiae, I. bucharica* and *I. reticulata*) the overwhelming majority found in today's gardens are Dutch hybrids (*Iris hollandica*). 'Hildegarde' is a Dutch hybrid with an average height of 60 cm (24 in) and a maximum height of 80–90 cm (31–35 in). Its bulbs are planted 10 cm (4 in) deep and the same distance apart for a compact grouping.

Iris 'Ideal' ◄
Family: *Iridaceae*
Height: 60 cm (24 in)

Among the many darker colored Dutch irises, 'Ideal' is prized for its flowers' subtle gray-blue (rather than purple) tones. To make sure that this beauty stands out in your garden, plant next to clusters of white or yellow irises.

Iris 'Professor ▶ Blaauw'

Family: *Iridaceae*
Height: 60 cm (24 in)

'Professor Blaauw' is an *Iris tingitana* variety with marvelous gentian blue flowers and a small, contrasting streak of golden yellow, subtly outlined in white, at the center of each fall. Its bulbs are sometimes "prepared" for early blooming, in which case 'Professor Blaauw' blooms slightly earlier than the other Dutch hybrids, which usually bloom in late spring to early summer. Unprepared bulbs,

on the other hand, bloom in mid-summer, or slightly later than the other Dutch hybrids.

Iris 'Madonna' ◀

Family: *Iridaceae*
Height: 60 cm (24 in)

The delicate, pinkish streak found on the inner side of each petal sets 'Madonna' apart from the other white and yellow irises. This detail, however, is best appreciated in cut flower arrangements. Although 'Madonna' is a Dutch hybrid, many excellent iris hybrids are available from other countries (particularly England and Germany) as well.

Iris reticulata ▶

Family: *Iridaceae*
Height: 15 cm (6 in)

Iris reticulata is another "rock garden iris" originally from Turkey and central Asia, where it grows spontaneously among the brushwood and in rocky soil, at elevations of 600–2,700 m (1,950–8,850 ft). The *I. reticulata* varieties differ from the Dutch hybrids in many ways; for example, *I. reticulata* blooms from late winter to early spring (much earlier than the Dutch hybrids) and is much smaller, with less ornate flowers. However, its flowers are still very lovely and fragrant, and ideal for rock gardens.

Iris 'Purple ◀ Sensation'

Family: *Iridaceae*
Height: 60 cm (24 in)

'Purple Sensation' has spectacular velvety, violet flowers and is one of today's most popular hybrids. Its long, thin, sage green leaves contrast handsomely with its dark purple blooms.

Iris reticulata ◄ 'Harmony'
Family: *Iridaceae*
Height: 15 cm (6 in)

While 'Harmony' has retained many of the original characteristics of the *I. reticulata* species, including its modest height, its violet-blue flowers are particularly beautiful and ornate. Each fall has a white patch, speckled with the same violet-blue as its petals, and a dark yellow, tonguelike stripe at its center.

Irises generally thrive in free-draining, alkaline soil, especially when planted in full sun. They grow especially well in rock gardens, and will continue to flower for many years, as long as they are not affected by any of the many bacteria or parasites that plague this genus.

Iris 'Royal ◄ Yellow'
Family: *Iridaceae*
Height: 60 cm (24 in)

'Royal Yellow' is a unique variety with vibrant, uniformly yellow flowers. The central, yellow, tonguelike blotch found on the falls of most irises is barely visible here, due to its similarly yellow petals. Plant 'Royal Yellow' with smaller flowers of contrasting colors (e.g., grape hyacinths) to draw attention to its golden blooms.

108
108

Iris

Iris 'Telstar' ▶

Family: *Iridaceae*
Height: 60 cm (24 in)

The classic purple and yellow color combination shared by many irises in this genus is also present in the 'Telstar' hybrid. Dutch irises (like 'Telstar') bloom earlier than the Spanish irises, and even earlier than the English irises, which often have spotted petals.

Iris 'White ▼ Wedgwood'

Family: Iridaceae
Height: 60 cm (24 in)

Although there are other colors in the Wedgwood family, iris connoisseurs usually pre-

fer 'White Wedgwood,' and consider it to be the most beautiful of all the whites in the *Iris* genus. Like other irises, 'White Wedgwood' can be propagated through bulb division in early fall. After it has bloomed, its bulbs require a warm, dry period, and must be stored in the appropriate environment once they have been extracted from the soil. Bulbous irises, however, are usually relatively hardy, and in milder climates can be left in the soil year-round.

Ixia
Corn lily

Ixia 'Mixed'
Family: *Iridaceae*
Height: 45 cm (18 in)

As its name suggests, this 'Mixed' variety produces flowers in a variety of contrasting colors (e.g., cream-colored flowers with pink-tipped petals, purple centers and yellow stamens). Although corn lilies are technically spring-blooming bulbs and should therefore be planted in the fall, they are often sold in the spring for summer blooming. After the first season, however, they tend to return to their natural growing season.

Ixia, or corn lilies, are native to South Africa, where today many different varieties are grown. The Ixia viridiflora varieties have pale green flowers with dark purple centers, while the Ixia maculata varieties have yellow or orange flowers with dark centers. Corn lilies are generally 30–45 cm (12–18 in) tall, and have long, grasslike leaves and tall flower spikes comprised of small, six-tepaled flowers that are approximately 3 cm (1 in) in diameter. Corn lilies bloom in late spring or early summer and are very cold sensitive. They must be grown indoors in all but the warmest climates. Indoors, plants should be kept in a sunny location, next to a window, and ideally between 7–10°C (45–50°F). Water generously until they bloom, and when their blooms have withered, extract the corms from the soil and store in a dry location until the next planting season.

Ixia

Ixiolirion

The only species of Ixiolirion *that is commonly cultivated is* Ixiolirion tataricum, *also called I. pallasii or I. montanum.* This species is originally from the steppes and mountainous slopes of southwest and central Asia and the Kashmir region of northern India, where it can be found growing at elevations ranging from 200–2,700 m (650–8,850 ft). Its bulbs are planted in the fall, 10 cm (4 in) deep and 7–15 cm (2½–6 in) apart. Ixiolirion grows most happily in full sun and free-draining soil, in a sheltered location near a garden wall or against the side of a house. Ixiolirion tataricum, *however, is a relatively hardy species that does not need fertilizing and can withstand temperatures as low as –15°C (5°F).* Ixiolirion *can also be propagated in the fall after the aboveground portion of the plant has withered by separating its bulbils or by planting its seeds indoors in the spring. Its bulbs must be removed from the soil in the fall and stored for the winter in dry peat at 10–15°C (50–60°F).*

Ixiolirion montanum

Family: *Amaryllidaceae*
Height: 35 cm (14 in)

Ixiolirion montanum is an elegant species, growing from a small egg-shaped bulb to a height of 40 cm (16 in), with long, grasslike leaves that appear in the spring before its flowers have bloomed. Its funnel-shaped, lavender flowers, usually 5 cm (2 in) wide, but sometimes 8–10 cm (3–4 in) wide, resemble clusters of tiny lilies. Despite its delicate perfume, *I. montanum* is not usually found in cut flower arrangements and does not respond particularly well to forcing.

Lachenalia

Originally from South Africa, the Lachenalia *genus (*Liliaceae *family) is made up of many smaller species of flowering bulbs, many of which are colorful late-winter or early-spring blooming varieties. The more common species, like* Lachenalia aloides *(or L. tricolor) and* Lachenalia bulbifera, *have round bulbs and racemes composed of 10 to 20 pendant, tubular flowers. Each individual flower is generally 2–3 cm (¾–1 in) long.* Lachenalia *reaches an average height of 20–30 cm (8–12 in).*

Lachenalia tricolor
Family: *Liliaceae*
Height: 20 cm (8 in)

Despite its modest size, *Lachenalia tricolor* makes a statement in almost any context, due to its striking bright orange-and-yellow flowers. However, it is a very cold-sensitive species that is usually grown indoors.

Plant bulbs 2–5 cm (¾–2 in) deep and 10 cm (4 in) apart, in soil that is equal parts sand, peat and potting soil. After planting, water once and store containers for the winter in a cold greenhouse or in any bright location that is well protected from the cold. The containers can be brought indoors as soon as the plants begin to grow. Their flowers will last longer if the temperature is not too warm. During the growth period, water and fertilize every two weeks. Water less after the plant has bloomed and stop watering completely during the summer. This dry period will allow the bulbs to rest. During the winter, store in a cold greenhouse. This species can be propagated by separating its bulbils during the summer. It is an excellent cut flower.

Lachenalia

Snowflakes are close relatives to the more common snowdrops (Galanthus), but have a differently shaped flower. Snowflakes are winter–spring bulbs that bloom from February to April or April to June (depending on the species).

Leucojum ◄ aestivum
Family: *Amaryllidaceae*
Height: 40 cm (16 in)

Although *Leucojum aestivum* is commonly known as the summer snowflake it actually blooms in spring. Each stem supports two to eight white, bell-shaped flowers that are approximately 1.5–2 cm (½–¾ in) in diameter with light green dots at the tip of each tepal. Summer snowflakes make wonderful cut flowers and respond well to forcing.

Leucojum vernum ◄
Family: *Amaryllidaceae*
Height: 20 cm (8 in)

The *Leucojum vernum,* or spring snowflake, actually begins flowering in February, but as its Latin name suggests (*vernum = of the spring*), it continues to flower through April. Spring snowflakes also have white flowers with light green dots at the tip of each tepal, but are smaller than summer snowflakes and only have one or two flowers per stem.

113

Leucojum

Muscari armeniacum
Family: *Liliaceae*
Height: 15 cm (6 in)

These little plants are native to Turkey and the Caucasus and Balkan regions where they grow in both grassy and rocky areas, at elevations of up to 2,000 m (6,560 ft). *Muscari armeniacum* grows from a scaly white bulb and has long, ribbonlike, sage-colored leaves and spears of tiny, blue, bell-shaped flowers with whitish rims. Its bulbs are planted in late summer or early fall, 10 cm (4 in) deep and 8–10 cm (3–4 in) apart.

115

Muscari, or grape hyacinths, are rather modest plants, particularly when it comes to their height, which rarely exceeds 30 cm (12 in). Their charming tiny purple flowers, and the fact that they are easy to grow, have made grape hyacinths popular garden protagonists; but beware—their wonderful fragrance and brightly colored, beadlike flowers attract bees! They are quickly pollinated, however, and soon transform into unique looking, pyramid-shaped fruit. Once the flowers have withered, do not cut the flower spikes if you want the seeds to mature. The ripe seeds will drop to the ground and cause the plants to spread. Grape hyacinths are also relatively hardy and can be left in the ground year-round.

Muscari ◄ 'Blue Spike'
Family: *Liliaceae*
Height: 15 cm (6 in)

'Blue Spike' is a variety of *M. armeniacum* that is typified by its particularly dense clusters of tiny, blue, sterile flowers. This plant requires no special care and even the least experienced gardener should have no trouble getting excellent results. Simply plant a handful of bulbs in the fall and wait for the spring to bring you clouds of blue flowers.

Muscari ◄ botryoides 'Album'
Family: *Liliaceae*
Height: 15 cm (6 in)

Muscari botryoides can be distinguished by its characteristically spade-shaped leaves that grow to a length of 15–20 cm (6–8 in). The variety 'Album' is known for its uncommon white flowers and is often used in cut-flower arrangements; there are violet-blue varieties as well. Grape hyacinths tend to spread quickly and can sometimes be a nuisance when spreading to unwanted sections of the garden. To prevent this from occurring, simply thin them out every few years.

Muscari

Muscari latifolium ◄
Family: *Liliaceae*
Height: 25 cm (10 in)

It is easy to tell this species from the other grape hyacinths because it is slightly taller and has reddish purple flowers that gradually darken towards the tip of each flower spike. Like other grape hyacinths, *Muscari latifolium* are not particularly cold-sensitive and are easily naturalized. They are also not usually prone to disease, but it is always a good idea to plant bulbs as soon as possible after purchasing them.

Muscari ► plumosum
Family: *Liliaceae*
Height: 30 cm (12 in)

The vivid, dark pink, branchlike flowers of *Muscari plumosum* are in sharp contrast with the other grape hyacinths. It is also the tallest species in the genus, sometimes exceeding 30 cm (12 in) in height. However, like other *Muscari*, it will grow happily in a sunny corner of the garden, in rich, moist, well-drained soil. *M. plumosum* is also perfect for rock gardens or along gravel paths, as long as the soil has been enriched with a long-lasting organic fertilizer.

Muscari

Narcissus

Narcissus 'Actaea'

Family: *Amaryllidaceae*
Height: 40 cm (16 in)

'Actaea' is a typical "poeticus" daffodil, derived from the *Narcissus poeticus* species. Poeticus daffodils have only one delicately fragrant flower per stem, and bloom slightly later than other types of daffodils. Its delicate flowers are 8–10 cm (3–4 in) wide and have white corollas with small, yellow, orange-rimmed coronas. Its bulbs are planted 15 cm (6 in) deep and 10 cm (4 in) apart. Poeticus daffodils also make perfect cut flowers.

There are over 50 naturally occurring species of daffodils and a great many more cultivated varieties. While most daffodils are native to the Mediterranean coastal countries of France, Italy, Spain, Portugal, Croatia and Greece, they can also be found growing naturally in Syria and in the hills of Austria and Switzerland.

The daffodil's flower is divided into two sections: the external "corolla," composed of six starlike lobes (or tepals) connected at their base, and the internal trumpet or cup-shaped "corona," so-called for its ridged, crownlike edges. The many varieties of daffodils are separated into 12 different divisions, based primarily on the shape and color of their flowers. Some varieties of daffodils have trumpet-shaped coronas, while others have coronas that are cup-shaped and more ornate than the corolla. The corona and the corolla are sometimes monochrome, but usually they are two different colors.

Narcissus ▲ 'Baby Moon'
Family: *Amaryllidaceae*
Height: 20 cm (8 in)

This "jonquilla" daffodil is not particularly cold-sensitive, but prefers a sunny spot in the garden away from the heavy shade of evergreen trees, or anywhere where there is little sun exposure. However, daffodils can be planted under any kind of tree that loses its leaves in the fall and does not grow new ones until mid-spring.

Narcissus ▼ 'Bridal Crown'
Family: *Amaryllidaceae*
Height: 25 cm (10 in)

"Double" daffodils have two corollas and a roselike corona, giving them twice as much flower as the standard daffodil. The light cream-colored corolla and soft orange corona of 'Bridal Crown' blend together instead of contrasting. Like most daffodils, 'Bridal

Crown' can withstand temperatures as low as −10°C (14°F). Its bulbs, however, do not like to sit in cold water during the winter months, so choose a free-draining corner of the garden, in sandy soil or on a slight slope.

Narcissus ▲ canaliculatus
Family: *Amaryllidaceae*
Height: 15 cm (6 in)

Narcissus canaliculatus is originally from the northern Mediterranean region and, along with the 'Geranium' variety, illustrated later in this chapter, falls into the "tazetta" division. While *N. canaliculatus* has smaller blooms than many of the other naturally occurring species of daffodils, each stem produces clusters of three to 12 fragrant flowers with pointed cream-colored tepals and golden yellow coronas. Like other daffodils, its bulbs can stay in the soil year-round.

To promote naturalizing, remove the dead flowers after they have withered, but do not cut its leaves; flowering bulbs use their leaves to collect the nutrients they need to survive the winter and produce next year's flowers.

Narcissus ◄ 'Dutch Master'

Family: *Amaryllidaceae*
Height: 40 cm (16 in)

This classic "trumpet" daffodil has one wonderfully fragrant, deep yellow, monochrome flower per stem, with a trumpetlike corona. To achieve long brushstrokes of color in the lawn, plant bulbs approximately 10–15 cm (4–6 in) apart, or for a more diffused effect, plant small clusters of three to four bulbs 30 cm (12 in) apart, and mix with other perennials.

Narcissus ► 'February Gold'

Family: *Amaryllidaceae*
Height: 40 cm (16 in)

'February Gold,' like all "cyclamineus" daffodils, is a *Narcissus cyclamineus* cultivar, with pendant, cyclamen-like flowers. The yellow flowers of 'February Gold' appear in early spring, making it one of the most precocious daffodils. Its bulbs are planted 15 cm (6 in) deep and the same distance apart. For best results, check the quality of your bulbs before planting. A healthy, high quality bulb is heavy and firm to the touch.

Narcissus ▶ 'Fortune'

Family: *Amaryllidaceae*
Height: 35 cm (14 in)

'Fortune,' like 'Flower Record,' is another "large-cupped" daffodil, but its soft apricot corolla and dark, creamy orange corona create a harmonious equilibrium that sets it apart from both the monochrome and the high-contrast varieties.

Narcissus ◀ 'Flower Record'

Family: *Amaryllidaceae*
Height: 35 cm (14 in)

Like all "large-cupped" daffodils, the corona of 'Flower Record' is proportionately larger than those found on other daffodils. 'Flower Record' is also one of the taller daffodils, and can reach a maximum height of 40 cm (16 in). It grows well both in containers and in the garden, and makes a lovely cut flower.

Narcissus ◄ 'Geranium'
Family: *Amaryllidaceae*
Height: 40 cm (16 in)

'Geranium' is strikingly similar to both *Narcissus canaliculatus* and 'Actaea' because it is a cross between a "tazetta" daffodil (like *N. canaliculatus*) and a "poeticus" daffodil (like 'Actaea'). Its wonderful perfume and multiple blooms (three to five per stem) have made it a garden favorite. 'Geranium' is easy to grow, but requires well-turned soil that is able to both retain moisture and drain excess water; these soil conditions can be achieved by adding humus and sand.

Narcissus ◄ 'Gold Ducat'
Family: *Amaryllidaceae*
Height: 40 cm (16 in)

This lovely flower is easily recognizable as a "double" daffodil. In the case of 'Gold Ducat' the overabundance of petals is accentuated by the fact that the petals of the corona and the corolla are united by the same golden yellow color, creating an almost roselike effect.

Narcissus

Narcissus ▶ 'Golden Harvest'

Family: *Amaryllidaceae*
Height: 40 cm (16 in)

The prominent corona of this uniformly golden cultivar makes 'Gold Harvest' easy to recognize as a "trumpet" daffodil. Like most daffodils, its bulbs are divided into two sections: the larger portion produces flowers in the spring, while the smaller portion produces only leaves the first year. Both portions begin to produce flowers in the second year.

Narcissus 'Hawera' ▶

Family: *Amaryllidaceae*
Height: 20 cm (8 in)

'Hawera' is a *Narcissus triandrus* cultivar (like all "triandrus" daffodils) with multiple flowers per stem. Each flower is lemon yellow and slightly pendant, with a shortened corona, made more visible by the slight upward projection of the corolla.

Narcissus ▲ 'Ice Follies'
Family: *Amaryllidaceae*
Height: 35 cm (14 in)

This "large-cupped" daffodil produces a single flower on each stem. Its creamy white flowers have a diameter of 8–10 cm (3–4 in) with lemon yellow coronas that gradually lighten during the season. This popular daffodil blooms in early spring and can be planted with some of the later bloomers for a longer continuous daffodil season.

Narcissus 'Jetfire' ◄
Family: *Amaryllidaceae*
Height: 20 cm (8 in)

'Jetfire' is another "cyclamineus" daffodil with bright yellow flowers and slightly darker yellow cups. It is among the first daffodils to bloom (early March) and can also be forced to bloom during the holiday season. For best results, fill a glass bowl with a thin layer of gravel (approximately 5 cm [2 in] deep) and place the bulbs on top—the closer they are together, the more beautiful the results. Next, cover the bulbs with gravel, leaving only the bulb tips showing; water, and place the container in a dark location, maintaining a constant temperature of 10°C (50°F) for approximately three weeks. At the end of this period the bulb roots should be clearly visible through the glass. When this occurs, move the container to a bright, relatively warm location and wait for the bulbs to bloom.

Narcissus ▼ 'Mount Hood'
Family: *Amaryllidaceae*
Height: 40 cm (16 in)

This "trumpet" daffodil has large ivory flowers with slightly darker coronas. It reaches a maximum height of 45 cm (18 in).

Narcissus ◄ 'Jack Snipe'
Family: *Amaryllidaceae*
Height: 20 cm (8 in)

This "cyclamineus" daffodil is easy to identify by its back-flared petals. 'Jack Snipe' is a daffodil of modest dimensions with lovely cream-colored and yellow flowers that grows particularly well in containers. Six to eight bulbs planted in a 30-cm (12 in) wide clay pot makes a charming spring display. In the garden, bulbs should be planted 10 cm (4 in) deep and the same distance (or less) apart.

Narcissus ▾ 'Rip Van Winkle'
Family: *Amaryllidaceae*
Height: 15 cm (6 in)

If it weren't for the bright yellow color of its flowers, this "double" daffodil would not look like a daffodil at all. Its corona and corolla are completely camouflaged by its many thin and pointed, tattered-looking petals, which almost make it look like a dahlia.

Narcissus ▴ 'Orangery'
Family: *Amaryllidaceae*
Height: 40 cm (16 in)

This cultivar has been placed in the "miscellaneous" division, reserved for those daffodils that do not fit the classifications of the other divisions. 'Orangery' has white flowers with vivid yellow centers and pairs nicely with early blooming herbaceous plants like *Euphorbia polychroma, Primula, Pulmonaria, Pulsatilla, Aubrieta* and *Alchemilla mollis*.

Daffodils can also be planted with late blooming hellebores or flowering trees and shrubs (especially those that bloom before growing their leaves), like *Magnolia stellata* and Japanese quince. Late season daffodils go well with *Pachysandra, Vinca* and *Lamiastrum*.

Narcissus 'Salome' ◄
Family: *Amaryllidaceae*
Height: 35 cm (14 in)

This delicate ivory-and-peach-colored, "large-cupped" daffodil is beautiful in cut-flower bouquets. However, daffodils are not always the best choice for mixed flower arrangements because their stems emit a particular mucilaginous substance that is not well tolerated by other kinds of flowers, causing them to wilt faster.

Narcissus 'Sir ► Winston Churchill'
Family: *Amaryllidaceae*
Height: 35 cm (14 in)

This "double" daffodil, dedicated to the great English statesman, has billowy, cream-colored petals with a vivid orange center. 'Sir Winston Churchill' is a favorite in cut-flower bouquets.

Narcissus

Narcissus 'Tahiti' ◄

Family: *Amaryllidaceae*
Height: 50 cm (20 in)

Among the many daffodils described in this section, this "double" daffodil is the tallest. 'Tahiti' also produces large and unique looking blooms that are approximately 10–12 cm (4–5 in) wide. Its voluminous flower has a lovely primrose corolla and fiery orange corona.

Like other daffodils of this size, 'Tahiti' should be planted 20 cm (8 in) deep and at least 15 cm (6 in) apart. Its bulbs must also be stored in a cool location, and kept in a paper bag to insulate them from the humidity. This method will prevent mold from growing and roots from forming before you are able to plant them.

Narcissus ◄ 'Tête-à-tête'

Family: *Amaryllidaceae*
Height: 20 cm (8 in)

In sharp contrast with the previous entry, this "miscellaneous" daffodil is one of the smallest, sometimes reaching a height of only 15 cm (6 in). However, 'Tête-à-tête' produces charming, golden yellow flowers and grows well in containers.

Narcissus

where they will act as the centerpiece to your composition.

Besides traditional flowerpots, daffodils can also be grown in wooden crates, copper pots, glass bowls, ceramic vases, plastic window boxes or almost any kind of container you can think of, as long as drainage holes have been provided.

Narcissus ▼ 'Van Sion'
Family: *Amaryllidaceae*
Height: 35 cm (14 in)

This strange "double" daffodil is the epitome of finding harmony in contrast. Its smooth outer petals are in stark opposition with its curly corona, and its golden yellow flowers contrast with its silvery green leaves.

Narcissus ▲ 'Thalia'
Family: *Amaryllidaceae*
Height: 35 cm (14 in)

This "triandrus" daffodil has two to three fragrant white flowers per stem, and is easy to grow in containers, provided the container is at least 25 cm

(10 in) deep. When planting daffodils in layers with other kinds of bulbs (e.g., crocuses, grape hyacinths and tulips), the daffodils should be placed on the bottom layer, so that they are covered with at least 15 cm (6 in) of soil. For best results, place daffodils at the center of the container,

Nectaroscordum

The Mediterranean nectaroscordums resemble the ornamental onions of the Allium genus. Like Allium, nectaroscordums have thick, bare stalks terminating in an umbel of small flowers. They also give off a slight onion scent when they are crushed or brushed against, although the Allium scent is more pungent. Nectaroscordums will thrive in the partial shade of a large tree, in moist, well-drained soil. They also naturalize and spread easily, but can sometimes be downright invasive! If they begin to spread to unwanted sections of the garden, simply thin them out occasionally. The two most common species of Nectaroscordum are Nectaroscordum siculum and Nectaroscordum bulgaricum; they are very similar and easily confused.

Nectaroscordum ◄ siculum
Family: *Liliaceae*
Height: 90 cm (35 in)

Nectaroscordum siculum resembles an ornamental onion, with its tall elegant stalks, often more than 90 cm (35 in) tall. It has long, green, basal leaves that wither after the plant has flowered and its bare stem supports a 30–45-cm (12–18-in) wide umbel. Each umbel is comprised of approximately 15 light (but not white), pendant, bell-shaped flowers with pale yellow, green and pink accents. Some varieties also have purplish red flowers. *N. siculum* flowers in late spring–early summer and grows well in ordinary garden soil. They also make excellent fresh or dried cut flowers.

Nectaroscordum

Ornithogalum ◄ balansae
Family: *Liliaceae*
Height: 10 cm (4 in)

Ornithogalum balansae is originally from northeastern Turkey, where it can be found growing naturally at elevations of over 2,500 m (8,200 ft). It is a dwarfish species with a maximum height of 10 cm (4 in) and is also a precocious, early spring bloomer. Each plant has two to three wide, lush, dark green leaves that bend back to make room for a short cluster of small white-and-green, star-shaped flowers.

133

Ornithogalum ◄ umbellatum
Family: *Liliaceae*
Height: 20 cm (8 in)

The Mediterranean *Ornithogalum umbellatum* or "star of Bethlehem" has thin, grasslike leaves and clusters of six to 20 star-shaped flowers. Its flowers are white with green stripes on the outer side of each of its six tepals. *O. umbellatum* naturalizes and spreads easily.

The Ornithogalum genus includes species from Mediterranean Europe, Western Asia and Sub-Saharan Africa, but only a few of these many varieties are commonly cultivated.

Ornithogalum grow happily in common garden soil as long as they are given proper drainage. The spring blooming species are usually smaller.

Oxalis

Oxalis, *the only genus in the* Oxalidaceae *family, differs from all of the other bulbous plants described in this book because, depending on its species,* Oxalis *can have rhizomes, tubers or tuberous roots.*

The splendid yellow Oxalis cernua *is native to South Africa, but most* Oxalis *are native to the Patagonian region of South America and the Falkland Islands.* Oxalis cernua *is also a typical spring bloomer, while other species, such as* Oxalis adenophylla *and* Oxalis deppei *are summer or fall bloomers.*

Oxalis cernua
Family: *Oxalidaceae*
Height: 25 cm (10 in)

The small size of the South African *Oxalis cernua* does not detract from the beauty of its vivid, slightly pendant, bell-shaped flowers that are double in some varieties. This low-growing species forms a carpet of shiny, palm-shaped, semi-succulent leaves, accented with bright yellow flowers which are 2–3 cm (¾–1 in) in diameter. It is a half-hardy species that can be planted outside only in regions with mild winters. In colder climates it can be grown in greenhouses, in containers that are at least 25 cm (10 in) wide. After it has bloomed, it can be propagated by separating its bulbils. Its bulbs are planted in spring or fall, 8–10 cm (3–4 in) deep.

Accidentally introduced on the island of Malta in the 18th century, *O. cernua* rapidly became naturalized and spread to southern Italy and the warmer regions of Europe. It grows best in a warm sheltered location, in full or partial sun, and free-draining soil enriched with peat or loam. In mild regions where *O. cernua* can be cultivated outside, cover with a thick layer of leaves during the winter season.

Oxalis

Puschkinia

This member of the Lili-aceae family is originally from the Middle East; although this region usually conjures images of hot, sunny weather, Puschkinia are actually found in the snowy mountain meadows and rocky regions of the Caucasus Mountains and Turkey, to 3,000 m (9,840 ft) in elevation. Puschkinia *resemble* Chionodoxa, *but have smaller, bell-shaped flowers that are sometimes white, depending on the variety. Plant in large groups for a more dramatic effect.*

Puschkinia libanotica
Family: *Liliaceae*
Height: 15 cm (6 in)

Sometimes called *Puschkinia scilloides* or the "striped squill," *Puschkinia libanotica* is a small plant not more than 20 cm (8 in) tall. It has a roundish bulb, ribbonlike leaves and clusters of six to12 bell-shaped flowers. Each flower is approximately 1.5 cm (½ in) long and has six pale blue tepals with darker blue stripes, except in the cultivar 'Alba,' which is pure white. The striped squill blooms from late winter to early spring and is a fairly hardy species that likes rock gardens and does well in small containers. It prefers sandy soil that is rich in humus, and a moderately sunny location. Its bulbs are planted in the fall, 8–10 cm (3–4 in) deep and 7–15 cm (2½–6 in) apart, depending on the desired visual effect. *P. libanotica* is relatively cold-resistant, but should nevertheless be covered with a layer of mulch during the winter. Propagate in the fall, either by separating its newly formed bulbils from the mother bulb (these bulbils should be replanted immedi-ately) or by planting its seeds. However, new plants grown from seed will not produce flowers for four years.

Scilla

Scilla ◄ mischtschenkoana
Family: *Liliaceae*
Height: 10 cm (4 in)

Scilla mischtschenkoana is a small plant with leaves that are shorter and wider than those found on other scillas. It also has loose clusters of wide, white, bell-shaped flowers, with light blue venation. Each flower is approximately 4 cm (1½ in) in diameter.

Scilla siberica ▼
Family: *Liliaceae*
Height: 15 cm (6 in)

This species has long, thin leaves and pendant, blue or white, bell-shaped flowers that are 2–3 cm (¾–1 in) wide. *Scilla siberica*, like *S. mischt-schenkoana*, grows well in containers.

There are many different species of scillas in the Liliaceae *family and all are of fairly modest dimensions. Scillas are late winter to early spring blooming bulbs with slightly different growing seasons for each species. They are also hardy plants that grow well in colder climates.*

Its bulbs are planted in the fall, 5–10 cm (2–4 in) deep and less than 10 cm (4 in) apart. Before plant-ing, choose a warm and sunny location and make sure that the soil is rich in humus and drains well. Bulbs can be left in the ground year-round and propagated at the end of the summer by separating the

bulbils from the larger bulb, or by planting the seeds. Scillas from seed will begin to flower after two to three years.

Scilla

Triteleia

The Triteleia *(or* Brodiaea*) genus contains species that are similar in appearance to the ornamental onions (*Allium*), but lack the odor. This genus includes species native to California, but only a few are available for cultivation.* Triteleia laxa *is one of the most commonly available species.*

Triteleia 'Queen Fabiola'
Family: *Liliaceae*
Height: 40 cm (16 in)

'Queen Fabiola' has rigid, bare stems that reach a maximum height of 50 cm (20 in) and ribbonlike leaves. Its terminal umbels are 4 cm (1½ in) wide and comprised of funnel-shaped, sapphire blue or violet flowers. 'Queen Fabiola' is a half-hardy cultivar that blooms in late spring or early summer and is an excellent cut flower. It grows happily in warm sunny locations, in very well-drained soil. Its corms are planted 10 cm (4 in) deep and the same distance apart.

Triteleia

Tulipa

Tulipa
TULIP

Tulips were once the world's most popular bulbs, if not the most popular of all spring-blooming garden flowers, and perhaps still are today. For many centuries tulips have been treasured for their distinctive cup-shaped flower, wide range of vivid colors and stiff, shiny petals. The classification of tulips has challenged generations of botanists and has been modified many times. Today, the 4,000 known varieties are grouped into 15 divisions, based on the flower's structure, blooming season and origin, with the last of the 15 divisions reserved for wild or naturally occurring species.

Tulipa 'Aladdin'
Family: *Liliaceae*
Height: 50 cm (20 in)

"Lily-flowered" tulips are characterized by their slightly outwardly curving, pointed petals, which, on 'Aladdin,' are brilliant red with lighter edges.

Tulipa

Tulipa 'Angélique' ▾
Family: *Liliaceae*
Height: 50 cm (20 in)

"Double late" tulips, as their name suggests, are late spring bloomers and have large double flowers that can reach a maximum diameter of 12 cm (5 in). Their full bloom has also earned them the name

Tulipa 'Apeldoorn' ▸
Family: *Liliaceae*
Height: 55 cm (22 in)

This "Darwin" tulip is 50–70 cm (20–28 in) tall with slender stems and blooms from mid to late spring. 'Apeldoorn' is one of the largest and most remarkable varieties of single-flowered tulips, with

Tulipa ▾ 'Apricot Beauty'
Family: *Liliaceae*
Height: 40 cm (16 in)

"Single early" tulips, as the name suggests, are small, single-flowered cultivars with

"peony flowering" tulips. The cultivar 'Angélique' can be identified by its pale to dark pink petals and its delicate fragrance (a rarity for tulips). Like most tulips, its bulbs are planted 15 cm (6 in) deep and 10 cm (4 in) apart.

a scarlet red flower that can reach 7 cm (2¾ in) in diameter. As with other Darwin tulips, its bulbs are planted some time from mid-September to mid-November, depending on local climate (sooner rather than later if the local climate is on the colder side).

Tulipa ▼ 'Brilliant Star'

Family: *Liliaceae*
Height: 30 cm (12 in)

'Brilliant Star' is another "single early" tulip that blooms in March and April. Its vermilion red flowers and short stems make it easy to identify. Like most tulips, 'Brilliant Star' must be planted in a sheltered location, well protected from the prevailing cold winds. Plant this variety in a sunny corner of the garden, at the base of a deciduous tree or in borders for a more conspicuous location.

cup-shaped blooms that open to 7 cm (2¾ in). Most hybrids do not grow more than about 20 cm (8 in) tall, although some varieties, like 'Apricot Beauty,' reach a maximum height of 40 cm (16 in). This hybrid gets its name from the lovely apricot color of its blooms.

Tulipa ◄ 'Couleur Cardinal'

Family: *Liliaceae*
Height: 35 cm (14 in)

'Couleur Cardinal' is a "triumph" tulip with classic, cardinal red flowers and the shortest stem in its class. It is also one of the few fragrant tulips.

Tulipa ◄ 'Dreaming Maid'

Family: *Liliaceae*
Height: 55 cm (22 in)

"Triumph" tulips are single-flowered, mid to late season bloomers with stems that are 35–60 cm (14–24 in) in length. 'Dreaming Maid' has delicate purplish pink flowers with white edges. It is also one of the tallest "triumph" tulips and makes an elegant cut flower.

Tulipa eichleri ►

Family: *Liliaceae*
Height: 30 cm (12 in)

"Species" tulips are found in the wild and are naturally occurring. *Tulipa eichleri* is species tulip of Asian origin, specifically from the Caucasus region of northern Iran, where it grows naturally in wheat fields and uncultivated slopes. It blooms from April to May. *Tulipa eichleri* is also called *Tulipa undulatifolia,* or "undulated-leafed tulip." It produces bright, mandarin red flowers.

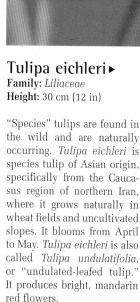

Tulipa

Tulipa ▼ 'Fancy Frills'
Family: *Liliaceae*
Height: 50 cm (20 in)

'Fancy Frills,' a late season "fringed" tulip, produces flowers that deepen in color from light pink at their base to dark pink at their tips. Like all "fringed" tulips, its petals have finely tattered edges, giving them a frilly, lacelike appearance.

Tulipa ◄ 'Flaming Parrot'
Family: *Liliaceae*
Height: 50 cm (20 in)

"Parrot" tulips can be distinguished from other kinds of tulips because their petal edges are jagged and serrated. The flowers of 'Flaming Parrot' are creamy yellow and streaked with satiny red markings.

Tulipa ▲ 'Estella Rijnveld'
Family: *Liliaceae*
Height: 50 cm (20 in)

This curious "parrot" tulip is easily identified, not only because of its ruffled and frayed petals, but also because of their complex, irregular, red-and-white designs. This elaborate color combination also makes 'Estella Rijnveld' immediately recognizable as belonging to the newest generation of hybrids—known for their vivacious colors.

Tulipa

Tulipa ▶
'Golden Apeldoorn'
Family: *Liliaceae*
Height: 55 cm (22 in)

'Golden Apeldoorn,' another "Darwin" tulip, has golden yellow petals with black and bronze star-shaped markings at their base; when the flower is open, its black anthers are also highly visible. Their long slender stems make this tulip an excellent cut flower.

Tulipa ▲
'Golden Parade'
Family: *Liliaceae*
Height: 55 cm (22 in)

The yellow flowers of 'Golden Parade,' another "Darwin" tulip, are a slightly different color from those of 'Golden Apeldoorn.' The color yellow is very prevalent among the thousands of varieties of tulips; it is one of the eternally classic solid colors, present in every shade imaginable.

Tulipa ▶
'Groenland'
Family: *Liliaceae*
Height: 60 cm (24 in)

Each stem of this "viridiflora" tulip produces one hourglass-shaped flower that is 8 cm (3 in) wide at its opening. Its petals are a luscious pink color, streaked vertically with apple green, giving the flower a feeling of spring freshness. While the base color can change from variety to variety, green markings are common to all viridiflora tulips.

Tulipa

Tulipa ◄ 'Heart's Delight'

Family: Liliaceae
Height: 15 cm (6 in)

"Kaufmanniana" tulips are *Tulipa kaufmanniana* cultivars with single flowers perched atop 15–25 cm (6–10 in) long stems. These tulips are also early bloomers. The long, slender petals may be one color or bicolor. 'Heart's Delight' produces pale-pink-and-red blooms.

Tulipa humilis ► violacea 'Black Base'

Family: *Liliaceae*
Height: 15 cm (6 in)

The *Tulipa humilis* species is native to the rocky slopes of Turkey and other Middle Eastern regions. Its Latin name *humilis* refers to its height, which does not exceed 10–15 cm (4–6 in). *T. humilis* cultivars, like the April-blooming 'Black Base,' are only slightly taller than the original species. Their bulbs are planted 10 cm (4 in) deep and 8 cm (3 in) apart, and can stay in the ground year-round.

Tulipa 'Kingsblood'

Family: *Liliaceae*
Height: 60 cm (24 in)

'Kingsblood' is a "single late" tulip with classic red blooms. "Single late" tulips bloom late in spring and have single, brightly colored, slender flowers, supported by stems that reach a maximum height of 70 cm (28 in). As with all bulbous plants, their leaves should never be removed after the plant has flowered, but left to wither naturally. Without their leaves, flowering bulbs can not perform photosynthesis and produce the nutrients they need to form new bulbs which feed next year's flowers.

Tulipa linifolia ◄
Family: *Liliaceae*
Height: 15 cm (6 in)

Tulipa linifolia is a small "species" tulip, generally only 10–20 cm (4–8 in) tall and perfect for growing in window boxes. Its scarlet red flower has light streaks at its base and on the outer side of its petals. Its leaves are narrow and grayish green with undulating edges. Its bulbs are planted 12 cm (5 in) deep and 7–8 cm (2½–3 in) apart.

Tulipa ►
'Lustige Witwe'
Family: *Liliaceae*
Height: 40 cm (16 in)

"Triumph" tulips are single-flowered, mid to late season bloomers of medium height. This cultivar, at 40 cm (16 in), is one of the shorter members of this group. 'Lustige Witwe' has white-edged, crimson flowers and, like all tulips, is easy to grow both indoors and out, as long as it is given plenty of sun, little water and a period of dry rest during the summer.

Tulipa ◄
'Monte Carlo'
Family: *Liliaceae*
Height: 30 cm (12 in)

"Double early" tulips begin flowering in mid-spring and have long, slender leaves and flower cups that can be 8 cm (3 in) in diameter. They also make excellent cut flowers and can be grown in mixed borders or in monochromatic groupings. 'Monte Carlo' is a "double early" tulip with a lemon yellow bloom.

Tulipa ►
'Orange Nassau'
Family: *Liliaceae*
Height: 30 cm (12 in)

'Orange Nassau,' another "double early" tulip, has bright red flowers with slightly lighter edges. Although we do not usually think of tulips as being flowers that can grow naturally and spread from year to year with little or no intervention, "double early" tulips are well suited to the job. Even if not all of the plants naturalize, you should have excellent results in two to three years.

Tulipa

Tulipa ◄ 'Page Polka'
Family: *Liliaceae*
Height: 45 cm (18 in)

"Triumph" tulips have become increasingly popular in recent years and the lovely pink flowers of 'Page Polka' show us why. All tulip bulbs must be planted in the fall and watered twice a week until the beginning of December; this practice will ensure that the bulbs are well hydrated when their roots begin to grow. Bulbs stop growing and become dormant during the winter, and begin to grow again as soon as the soil temperature begins to warm.

Tulipa ◄ 'Peach Blossom'
Family: *Liliaceae*
Height: 30 cm (12 in)

'Peach Blossom' is a "double early" tulip with expressive, antique pink flowers, streaked lightly with green and white. Early tulips bloom at the same time as many other types of flowering bulbs, and by taking advantage of these synchronized blooming periods, different colors and varieties can be used to create a garden that is always in full bloom. For example, tulips pair nicely with *Muscari armeniacum, Narcissus poeticus recurvus* or *Anemone blanda* in borders.

Tulipa

Tulipa praestans ▶ 'Fusilier'

Family: *Liliaceae*
Height: 25 cm (10 in)

The central Asian *Tulipa praestans* produces up to five flowers on each stem. Because of this unique ability *T. praestans* has played a central role in the creation of the so-called "multiflowered" tulips. 'Fusilier' is a "multiflowered" variety with wide, sage-colored leaves and large brilliant red flowers perched atop 25–30 cm (10–12 in) stems.

Tulipa ◀ 'Prinses Irene'

Family: *Liliaceae*
Height: 35 cm (14 in)

Its delicate fragrance (a rarity for tulips) and unique orange-and-purple petals has made this early spring bloomer one of the most popular varieties. It is often found in flowerbeds and cut-flower arrangements. For a lovely contrast, surround 'Prinses Irene' with a carpet of forget-me-nots.

Tulipa

Tulipa 'Purissima'

Family: *Liliaceae*
Height: 40 cm (16 in)

"Fosteriana" tulips—the hybrids of *T. fosteriana* with other species, such as *T. greigii* and *T. kaufmanniana*—are mid-season bloomers with single flowers that can reach a maximum diameter of 12 cm (5 in). Its stems range from 15 to 45 cm (6 to 18 in) in height. The hybrid 'Purissima' has bright white flowers and contrasting dark green leaves.

Tulipa ◄
'Red Riding Hood'
Family: *Liliaceae*
Height: 20 cm (8 in)

"Greigii" tulips are *T. greigii* cultivars that produce 10-cm (4-in) wide flowers in late spring–early summer. Their characteristic silvery green leaves with violet stripes make them easy to identify. 'Red Riding Hood' is a "greigii" hybrid with scarlet red blooms.

Any bulbs that can not be planted immediately should be stored in a dry, cool location to prevent mold from growing.

Tulipa saxatilis ►
Family: *Liliaceae*
Height: 20 cm (8 in)

Tulipa saxatilis, native to the meadows and rocky hillsides of the island of Crete, grows happily in hot sun and well-drained soil. Each stem produces up to four delicate pink flowers with yellow centers. Its wide, linear leaves are light green. It propagates by means of stolons.

Tulipa ◄ 'Spring Green'
Family: *Liliaceae*
Height: 50 cm (20 in)

The typical green streaks that run vertically down the outside of its petals make 'Spring Green' easy to identify as a "viridiflora" tulip. Like all tulips, this cultivar requires a dry, dormant summer period. If the tulips have been planted alone, simply stop watering after the leaves have withered, but if they have been planted with other flowers that need watering during the hot summer months, the bulbs should be removed from the soil.

Tulipa tarda ◄
Family: *Liliaceae*
Height: 15 cm (6 in)

The Asian *Tulipa tarda* is a unique species of dwarf tulip with five to six star-shaped flowers per stem. Each flower is yellow with white edges and has a maximum diameter of 5 cm (2 in). This species is suitable for borders and rock gardens and grows easily in containers, but prefers rich, freely draining, dry soil.

Tulipa 'Toronto' ▸

Family: *Liliaceae*
Height: 25 cm (10 in)

This "greigii" tulip is appreciated for its uniformly vermilion flower that is slightly green-tinted at its base. Winter rain and snow usually provides enough moisture so that tulips do not need watering during the winter months, but if the winter has been particularly dry, the bulbs may need to be watered towards the end of the season to prevent dehydration. As soon as the plants begin to grow again, they should be watered twice a week.

Tulipa ◂ turkestanica

Family: *Liliaceae*
Height: 15 cm (6 in)

Tulipa turkestanica is native to the Pamir Mountain region of central Asia (the border between China and Tajikistan) where it can be found growing on jagged slopes, 1,800–2,500 m (5,900–8,200 ft) in elevation. It has small, star-shaped, white flowers with yellow throats and light grayish pink markings on the outer side of each petal. Its height ranges from 10 to 25 cm (4 to 10 in).

Tulipa urumiensis ◄

Family: Liliaceae
Height: 15 cm (6 in)

Tulipa urumiensis is a "species" tulip with star-shaped flowers, like those of *T. tarda,* that are uniquely yellow and bronze-colored. It is a dwarfish variety with a delicate perfume. It is fairly easy to grow both indoors and out, as long as it is provided with the standard freely draining soil and sunny location.

Tulipa ►
'West Point'

Family: Liliaceae
Height: 50 cm (20 in)

Its long, slightly outward fanning, pointed petals make 'West Point' (like 'Aladdin'), easy to identify as a "lily-flowered" tulip. This cultivar blooms around April or May and has slender, primrose yellow flowers. When planting a large area, prepare the soil by eliminating all residual vegetation and breaking up any large clumps of earth. For a nice visual effect, plant lower growing herbaceous plants between each bulb.

SUMMER BULBS

Achimenes

The South American Achimenes is a herbaceous perennial with horizontally growing stems that are approximately 30 cm (12 in) long and oval leaves that are sometimes red-spotted. Its flowers are 5 cm (2 in) in diameter and funnel-shaped with five large, irregular lobes.

Achimenes longiflora
Family: *Gesneriaceae*
Height: 20 cm (8 in)

Achimenes longiflora is a species that grows well in greenhouses. It loves the light, but can not be exposed to direct sun and can survive outdoors only in very warm and sheltered locations. Its tubers are planted in early spring, 3 cm (1 in) apart and lightly covered with 2–3 cm (¾–1 in) of peat-enriched soil. Irrigation should be moderate at first and abundant during its peak growth period. It can be propagated by seed or by separating its newly formed tubers when dormant.

Agapanthus
AFRICAN LILY

The name Agapanthus means "flower of love" in Greek, but today this South African native is known mostly for its hardiness. Clusters of numerous funnel- or bell-shaped flowers sit atop long, bare stems, surrounded by tufts of dark green linear leaves. Agapanthus has tuberous roots and blooms in midsummer.

Agapanthus ▶ africanus

Family: *Liliaceae*
Height: 70 cm (28 in)

Native to the Cape Provinces of South Africa, *Agapanthus africanus* is a half-hardy species that does well in temperate climates if planted in a sunny location and in fertile, well-drained soil. Its tuberous roots are planted in the spring and produce blue flowers in July and August. There are pink, white and bicolor varieties as well.

Agapanthus ◀ campanulatus

Family: *Liliaceae*
Height: 60 cm (24 in)

Agapanthus campanulatus has lovely round inflorescences that range from 15–30 cm (6–12 in) in diameter and are composed of 10 to 30 white, pale blue or lavender, trumpet-shaped flowers. Its tuberous roots are planted 3 cm (1 in) deep and grow well in containers. Its strong roots, however, have a tendency to crack containers and should, therefore, be repotted every season.

Amaryllis
NAKED LADY

Amaryllis belladonna 'Parkeri'

Family: *Amaryllidaceae*
Height: 80 cm (31 in)

The different varieties of *Amaryllis belladonna* prefer mild Mediterranean climates and full or partial sun. Their flowers appear in late summer when the foliage has withered completely (hence the common name "naked lady"). These plants grow well in rich, light, freely draining soil. The bulbs are planted in late summer, 20 cm (8 in) deep and the same distance apart, and can be grown in containers, provided they are of adequate size, and making sure that the top of the bulb is pointing upwards. Water generously and fertilize periodically until the leaves begin to wither; when this occurs, stop watering until the first flowers appear. *Amaryllis belladonna* can be propagated during its dormant season and, although it is not particularly delicate, it must be provided with a winter covering, especially in colder climates. A thick winter mulch of dry leaves and straw should be more than adequate protection.

The graceful South African Amaryllis belladonna *or "naked lady" is the only "true amaryllis," and should not be confused with the South American* Hippeastrum, *which has been given the common name "amaryllis."* Amaryllis belladonna *has large, pear-shaped bulbs and four to eight shiny, linear leaves that range from 20–50 cm (8–20 in) in length. Its straight stems are approximately 60–90 cm (24–35 in) tall and support umbels of five to 12 large, fragrant, trumpet-shaped, pink or white flowers with yellow throats. Each flower is approximately 8 cm (3 in) wide.*

Amaryllis

Anemone

Anemones are members of the family Ranunculaceae, *which includes both spring-blooming varieties, like* Anemone blanda, *and summer bloomers, like* Anemone coronaria *described in this section.*

Anemone ◄ coronaria 'De Caen'
Family: *Ranunculaceae*
Height: 30 cm (12 in)

'De Caen' produces wonderful red, white, pink or light blue double blooms between May and July. It requires a warm and sunny climate (Mediterranean or similar) and will not survive long in cold regions. Its bulbs are planted 5 cm (2 in) deep and 10–15 cm (4–6 in) apart.

Anemone ◄ coronaria 'St. Brigid'
Family: *Ranunculaceae*
Height: 30 cm (12 in)

Although the many varieties of *Anemone coronaria* are very similar to one another, 'St. Brigid' has more petals, giving it a fuller-looking bloom. *A. coronaria* are also called "florists' anemones" and are commonly used as cut flowers.

Arum

The genus Arum *contains many unique bulbs that brighten our gardens with their blooms almost year-round (spring, summer and fall). These plants are highly appreciated for their decorative foliage and bright red poisonous berries that ripen in the fall. From late spring until early summer they also produce attractive clusters of tiny flowers.*

Arum italicum
Family: *Araceae*
Height: 35 cm (14 in)

The oval tubers of *Arum italicum* are planted 8 cm (3 in) deep and 10 cm (4 in) apart. In regions with mild winters, the foliage, which develops in the fall, will last right through the winter. During its blooming season it produces a long, club-shaped inflorescence encircled by a winding yellow spathe. Striking clusters of bright, shiny, reddish orange berries ripen in the fall.

Arum

Babiana

The plants in this genus of Iridaceae *resemble freesias and are native to South Africa where they can be found blooming on hillsides and in grassy meadows.* Babiana *is also known as the "baboon flower," because its corms are a favorite food of baboons ("babanier" means "baboon" in Afrikaans). Baboon flowers are delicate and require a warm climate and fertile soil that is high in organic matter. Plant in a sheltered location in full sun.*

Babiana rubrocyanea
Family: *Iridaceae*
Height: 25 cm (10 in)

Each short flower spike of *Babiana rubrocyanea* holds five to 10 trumpet-shaped, reddish purple flowers that are 4–5 cm (1½–2 in) in diameter. Baboon flowers can not tolerate the cold so their corms must be extracted from the soil during the winter or covered with a layer of mulch, depending on local climate.

Babiana

Begonia

While the most common begonias have fibrous roots, some varieties have tubers and are therefore considered bulbous plants.

Begonia bertinii ▶
Family: *Begoniaceae*
Height: 30 cm (12 in)

Begonia bertinii, along with the other begonias described in this section, falls into the category of *Begonia tuberhybrida* or "tuberous begonia." This species has delicate red flowers and is easily grown in containers.

163

Begonia crispa ▶
Family: *Begoniaceae*
Height: 25 cm (10 in)

This variety of tuberous begonia gets its name from the wrinkled or puckered texture of its petals, which are yellow towards their centers and bright red along their edges. As with the other tuberous begonias, its tubers are planted 5 cm (2 in) deep and 25 cm (10 in) apart.

Begonia

Begonia double ▶

Family: *Begoniaceae*
Height: 25 cm (10 in)

These hybrids, commonly called "double begonias," have white, yellow, pink, orange or red flowers. These colors are common to tuberous begonias, but shades of blue are completely absent from the begonia palette.

Double begonias have short, reddish green stems with alternating, irregular, fleshy, rugose leaves. Tuberous begonias prefer rich, well-drained soil with high organic content and should be fertilized with well-rotted manure.

Begonia ◀ fimbriata

Family: *Begoniaceae*
Height: 25 cm (10 in)

Begonia fimbriata is particularly valued for its brightly colored double flowers with ruffled petals. Its tubers are planted indoors in March or April, grown at a temperature of approximately 18°C (64°F) and transplanted into the garden after two months. At the onset of the cold season, its tubers should be removed from the soil, left to dry in a warm location, wiped clean of loose soil and stored in bags of peat at 4–10°C (39–50°F).

Begonia

Begonia ◄ marmorata

Family: *Begoniaceae*
Height: 25 cm (10 in)

The *Begonia marmorata* or "marbled begonia" has reddish pink and white marbled petals. Although this particular variety is rather small, some begonia hybrids can reach a maximum height of 60 cm (24 in). Its tubers are planted in full or partial sun, in a sheltered position, and must be watered generously. They can be propagated by stem cuttings or by seeds planted indoors in January (for June flowers).

Begonia ► multiflora maxima

Family: *Begoniaceae*
Height: 20 cm (8 in)

Tuberous begonias bloom from mid-summer to early fall (July to October) and their flowers can be pendant, marbled, bordered or camellia-shaped. *Begonia multiflora maxima* produces vibrant red, yellow, pink and white flowers, and like the other varieties, can not tolerate the cold, but grows well both indoors and out when given the proper growing conditions.

Canna

Canna 'Lucifer' ◄
Family: *Cannaceae*
Height: 60 cm (24 in)

Although this Canna is a "dwarf" variety, don't let that description fool you: 'Lucifer' can still grow to be 60–70 cm (24–28 in) tall! 'Lucifer' only seems dwarfish when compared to the classic cannas—which commonly reach a height of 1 m (3¼ ft)—or the giant cannas—which some-

166

Cannas are native to South America and have large, rootlike rhizomes. They have oval or spade-shaped leaves, generally 30–60 cm (12–24 in) long, and spiky inflorescences, with a cluster of flowers at each outgrowth.

Cannas have enjoyed a renaissance in recent years, both because they are relatively easy to grow and because new varieties with bright flowers and interesting foliage are now more widely available. Classic cherry red flowers or more exotic shades of pink,

yellow and orange grow along tall, thick stalks; their beauty is enhanced by the presence of very large and ornate stamens. However, their lush green leaves with copper and emerald reflections and delicate yellow venation make cannas attractive even when they are not in bloom.

Canna

times reach 2 m (6½ ft) in height. Dwarf cannas are summer-fall bloomers and their smaller size makes them well suited to growing in pots. Plant bulbs 8–10 cm (3–4 in) deep and up to 40 cm (16 in) apart.

Canna ▼
'The President'

Family: *Cannaceae*
Height: 90 cm (35 in)

'The President,' a classic "green-leafed" canna, has extraordinary crimson flowers and is usually about 1 m (3¼ ft)

tall. It blooms from July to November and grows happily in sunny spots and fertile soil mixed with sand and well-rotted manure. For more vibrantly colored flowers, apply potassium and phosphorus fertilizers during the growing season.

Canna 'Wyoming' ▲

Family: *Cannaceae*
Height: 90 cm (35 in)

'Wyoming' is a classic "red-leafed" canna with fiery orange flowers and, like 'The President,' it also blooms from July to November. Despite its large

size, 'Wyoming' grows happily in containers, as long as they are large enough for its rhizomes to be planted 10 cm (4 in) deep and 40 cm (16 in) apart. Like all foliage-heavy plants, 'Wyoming' must be watered generously, especially if the weather is dry or windy.

Commelina

Commelina coelestis

Family: *Commelinaceae*
Height: 45 cm (18 in)

Commelina coelestis, the blue spiderwort and the day-flower, all one and the same plant, is relatively easy to order from the major bulb catalogs. *Commelina* is native to Mexico and falls into the typical summer blooming period (July and August) which sometimes begins in late spring (June). Its flowers are varying shades of violet blue, illuminated by its vibrant yellow reproductive organs, which are plainly visible when the flower is fully open. Its bulbs are planted 10 cm (4 in) deep and the same distance apart in full sun and moist soil with adequate drainage.

Commelina is unique in that it is the only member of the Commelinaceae family presented in this book. Generally of medium height, 50–60 cm (20–24 in) tall, Commelina have tuberous roots that branch out irregularly, with some sections longer and more developed than others.

Convallaria
LILY-OF-THE-VALLEY

Convallaria majalis *(majalis = May)*, or lily-of-the-valley, grows spontaneously in most of Europe and North America. It is a typical flower of the woodland underbrush and is perfect for that cool, partially shady spot in the lawn. Its rhizomes are planted at the end of autumn, close together and just below the surface, in moist, humus-rich soil.

Convallaria majalis 'Alba'
Family: *Liliaceae*
Height: 20 cm (8 in)

Lilies-of-the-valley have two flat, bright green leaves that wrap partially around a spike of six to 12 pendant, white, bell-shaped flowers. The fragrant *Convallaria majalis* blooms in late spring and grows well in containers.

Crinum

Crinum are of tropical origin and require growing conditions that reproduce their natural environment. However, some varieties, particularly **Crinum powellii**, are hardy enough to be grown outdoors in parts of North America and Europe. Despite their large size, crinums should be grown in containers so they can be brought indoors during the winter months, when the bulbs are dormant.

Crinum powellii
Family: *Amaryllidaceae*
Height: 100 cm (39 in)

These large bulbs are planted in spring, 25–30 cm (10–12 in) deep and spaced well apart. *Crinum powellii* prefers fertile, well-drained soil and a warm and sunny location. It blooms in July and August and is generally 50–100 cm (20–39 in) tall, depending on the variety. Its umbrella-like pink or white inflorescences are comprised of 10 trumpet-shaped flowers and are generally 15 cm (6 in) long.

Crocosmia

Crocosmia *are originally from South Africa, but some species have now been naturalized in Europe as well, particularly along the Atlantic Coast.* Crocosmia crocosmiflora, *popular for its hardiness and wide range of colors,* was the first species to be exported to Europe, and for a long period of time the "European" crocosmias were almost exclusively hybrids of this species. However, other species, like Crocosmia masonorum *and its many hybrids, have since gained popularity. While hybrids differ in color and height, they have very similar planting requirements. There are many naturally occurring species of* Crocosmia, *but the most commonly grown varieties are cultivars.*

Crocosmia 'Emily McKenzie'
Family: *Iridaceae*
Height: 50 cm (20 in)

'Emily McKenzie,' like most *Crocosmia,* can reach a maximum height of 50–60 cm (20–24 in). It blooms from around July to September, producing tall spikes of red and orange flowers with long visible stamens. *Crocosmia* bloom progressively, starting with the lowest flowers on the stem. Its corms are planted 10 cm (4 in) deep and the same distance apart.

Crocosmia ◄ 'Lucifer'

Family: *Iridaceae*
Height: 60 cm (24 in)

While similar to 'Emily McKenzie,' 'Lucifer' has scarlet red, almost purple flowers that are excellent in cutflower arrangements, and are long lasting when adequately cared for in the garden.

In colder climates its corms must be removed from the soil before the first frost and dried and stored until spring. In milder climates, its corms can be left in the ground yearround so long as they are covered with a winter mulch.

Crocosmia ◄ masonorum

Family: *Iridaceae*
Height: 60 cm (24 in)

Crocosmia masonorum is considered by many enthusiasts to be the most beautiful species in the genus. It generally reaches 60–70 cm (24–28 in) in height, making it slightly taller than most varieties. It also has longer, spearlike leaves, and between July and September it produces tall spikes of orange flowers that are 3 cm (1 in) wide. *C. masonorum* is also a relatively hardy species that requires fertile, freely draining soil and a warm sunny location. Fertilize and water regularly throughout the summer.

Crocosmia

Curcuma

Curcuma alismatifolia

Family: *Zingiberaceae*
Height: 60 cm (24 in)

Curcuma alismatifolia, also called the Siam tulip because of its tulip-shaped bloom, is an exotic plant that can be grown outdoors only in the mildest regions of North America and Europe. However, the Siam tulip grows well in containers and can, therefore, be grown almost anywhere indoors. Delicate pink flowers, similar to double tulips, bloom from July to September amid pale green foliage. It can reach a height of 70 cm (28 in). Its tuberous roots are planted 5 cm (2 in) deep and spaced approximately 15 cm (6 in) apart.

172

Curcuma

As is evident from the examples presented in this book, most bulbs, or rather most bulbs that are widely available, belong to a very restricted number of families, especially Liliaceae, Iridaceae *and* Amaryllidaceae. *However, there are many other, less common families of bulbs that are very popular with bulb enthusiasts and are relatively easy to find with a little extra effort.* Bignoniaceae, Compositeae, Colchicaeae *and* Zingiberaceae *(to which the* Curcuma *genus belongs) are all examples of some of the lesser-known bulb families that deserve our attention.*

Cyclamen

The Cyclamen *genus in-cludes both winter–spring varieties, like* Cyclamen coum *described in the first half of this survey, and summer–fall bloomers, like the Mediterranean* Cycla-men hederifolium, *which blooms from late summer (August–September) to early fall (October). Like their spring-blooming rela-tives,* C. hederifolium *are of modest size—only 10 cm (4 in) tall.*

Cyclamen hederifolium
Family: *Primulaceae*
Height: 10 cm (4 in)
:

Cyclamen hederifolium, or "ivy-leaved" cyclamen, grows naturally in the Mediter-ranean region of southern Italy, in the partial shade of the woodland underbrush. It prefers partial shade and light humus-rich soil, and each short stem bears a sin-gle, scentless pink flower. Its tubers are planted in mid-summer, 5 cm (2 in) deep and 10–15 cm (4–6 in) apart.

Cyclamen

Cyrtanthus

The Cyrtanthus *or* Vallota *genus belongs to the family* Amaryllidaceae *and is native to South Africa. It can be grown outdoors only in regions with frost-free winters, but it grows well in containers and can, there-fore, be grown indoors or in greenhouses almost any-where. The several species of* Cyrtanthus *(including* Cyrtanthus elatus*) differ only in color and height, which ranges from 30–60 cm (12–24 in).*

Cyrtanthus elatus
Family: *Amaryllidaceae*
Height: 35 cm (14 in)

Cyrtanthus elatus produces pink, funnel-shaped blooms in July and August. Its bulbs are planted 15 cm (6 in) deep and the same distance apart. Water generously and fertilize with liquid fertilizer during the growing season, gradu-ally tapering off towards the end of the season.

Cyrtanthus

Dahlia

Dahlia

Dahlia 'Alabama' ◄
Family: *Compositae*
Height: 25 cm (10 in)

Dahlias are grown primarily for the beauty of their blooms, which are actually clusters of many small, elongated, petal-like florets which, in this variety, are double and bright yellow.

There are approximately 30 naturally occurring species of dahlias—many of which are rarely cultivated—and a few thousand hybrids. Dahlia hybrids are difficult to classify, and classifications often vary depending on source. Dahlias were named after the Swedish botanist and student of Linnaeus, Andreas Dahl in 1789, by the curator of the Royal Botanical Gardens in Madrid.

Dahlia ◄ 'Alfred Grille'
Family: *Compositae*
Height: 100 cm (39 in)

This beautiful "cactus" dahlia is salmon pink with a luminous yellow center. Dahlias vary considerably in height from one variety to the next. 'Alfred Grille,' for example, is almost a meter (3¼ ft) tall, while 'Alabama' only reaches a height of about 25 cm (10 in). Other varieties top off at 2 m (6½ ft).

Dahlia

Dahlia ◄ 'Arabian Night'
Family: *Compositae*
Height: 100 cm (39 in)

This variety of "decorative" dahlia is easily identified by its oxblood, almost black, flowers. Like all dahlias, 'Arabian Night' has light or dark brown tuberous roots (often simply called "tubers") with three to five outgrowths. The tubers are planted 10 cm (4 in) deep with the branches pointing down and covered with 2–3 cm (about 1 in) of soil, leaving the buds uncovered. A healthy tuberous root should be firm to the touch; if it is soft or mushy, the inner tissues have degenerated.

Dahlia ◄ 'Autumn Fairy'
Family: *Compositae*
Height: 35 cm (14 in)

This variety of "decorative" dahlia has dense double flowers with slightly concave petals. Its bloom is bright orange at its center, gradually fading to a lighter orange towards its outer edges. Like all dahlias, 'Autumn Fairy' has no fragrance.

Dahlia ▶
'Bergers Rekord'
Family: *Compositae*
Height: 100 cm (39 in)

'Bergers Rekord' is "semi-cactus" dahlia of medium height, but its bright purplish red flowers are what make it stand out in a crowd. Like all dahlias, it loves the sun and can not tolerate late-spring or winter frost. To avoid cold damage, make sure the last frost date has passed before planting, and choose a sunny location sheltered from the prevailing winds.

Dahlia ◀
'Bishop of Llandaff'
Family: *Compositae*
Height: 80 cm (31 in)

'Bishop of Llandaff' is one of the so-called "peony" dahlias with semidouble flowers and open centers. It has dark, elegant, uniformly red flowers and particularly decorative foliage. 'Bishop Llandaff' is an antique cultivar—first cultivated in 1927—that continues to enjoy success among today's dahlia lovers.

Dahlia ▶ 'Ellen Houston'
Family: *Compositae*
Height: 40 cm (16 in)

When compared with other dahlias, 'Ellen Houston' is smaller than average, sometimes less than 40 cm (16 in) tall, but its deliciously bright red blooms have no trouble grabbing attention both in the garden or in a stunning window box arrangement.

Dahlia 'Blusette' ▲
Family: *Compositae*
Height: 50 cm (20 in)

'Blusette' is a medium-sized "peony" dahlia (or "waterlily" dahlia, depending on the source) that rarely exceeds 50 cm (20 in) in height. Like most dahlias, 'Blusette' blooms from midsummer till fall. Its magenta flowers have bright yellow cores and a streak of ruby red down the center of each petal.

Dahlia 'Duet' ▶
Family: *Compositae*
Height: 80 cm (31 in)

This "decorative" dahlia has relatively large double blooms, with wide petals that gradually taper to a point at their tips, and are sometimes slightly undulating. Each flower is dark red, almost purple at its center and white at its edges: these two contrasting colors "duet" in this cultivar.

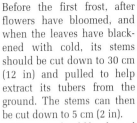

Before the first frost, after flowers have bloomed, and when the leaves have blackened with cold, its stems should be cut down to 30 cm (12 in) and pulled to help extract its tubers from the ground. The stems can then be cut down to 5 cm (2 in).

The roots should be cleaned of soil and hung upside down to dry; this position will force all of the moisture out of the tubers. They can then be placed in paper bags and stored in a dark, cool and dry location. This can be done with all dahlias. As an alternative, tubers can also be stored in boxes and lightly covered with a mixture of soil and sand.

Dahlia 'Eveline' ▼
Family: *Compositae*
Height: 100 cm (39 in)

'Eveline' is a beautiful white dahlia with a delicate, evanescent pink perimeter and center.

Dahlia ▼
'Garden Wonder'
Family: *Compositae*
Height: 65 cm (26 in)

'Garden Wonder' is a medium-sized "decorative" dahlia, with large, fiery red blooms. All medium to large dahlias require support stakes (bamboo canes work nicely) to keep them from falling over as they grow. However, instead of adding the stakes as needed, develop the habit of setting them out as you plant your

Dahlia ▲
'Franz Kafka'
Family: *Compositae*
Height: 80 cm (31 in)

This is a typical "pompon" dahlia, a term which accurately describes its ball-shaped, fully double bloom. It is relatively small when compared to other dahlias, but its blunt, lavender petals create a dramatic geometric display—like many tiny cones. Planting time depends on local climate: in mild climates, begin planting around the beginning of April, and in colder regions, wait until late April or even May to avoid risking late frost damage.

tubers, before covering the tubers with soil. This practice will keep you from damaging your dahlias by unwittingly spearing the hidden underground tubers with the support stakes.

Dahlia ◄
'Jeanne d'Arc'
Family: *Compositae*
Height: 120 cm (47 in)

This lovely "semi-cactus" dahlia consistently grows more than

1 m (3¼ ft) tall. Its delicately colored flower gradually and harmoniously blends from yellow at its center to ivory and pink at its outer edges.

Dahlia ▶
'Little Tiger'
Family: *Compositae*
Height: 50 cm (20 in)

Other than the complete absence of all colors on the blue-violet end of the spectrum, dahlias come in a seemingly endless variety of colors. This red-and-white color combination is reminiscent of 'Duet,' but in 'Little Tiger,' red clearly dominates over white, which is evident only at the flower's very outer edge.

Dahlia ◀
'Kelvin Floodlight'
Family: *Compositae*
Height: 90 cm (35 in)

This "decorative" dahlia has radiant yellow blooms that, like most dahlias, make excellent cut flowers. For one large bloom, simply eliminate the lateral buds or, for many smaller blooms, remove the tallest bud along with a piece of stem about 10 cm (4 in) long.

Dahlia ◄
'Nescio'
Family: *Compositae*
Height: 80 cm (31 in)

The sober ruby red color of this "pompon" dahlia seems to belie its lighthearted category name. Like all dahlias, 'Nescio' is not picky and grows well in all types of soil, from rich and fertile to impoverished and sandy.

Dahlia ◄
'Onesta'
Family: *Compositae*
Height: 110 cm (43 in)

This cultivar produces spectacular magenta, almost red, blooms. 'Onesta' is a large dahlia, usually more than a meter (3–3½ ft) tall. While it is true that dahlias are not overly demanding, consistent growth can be promoted by adding natural fertilizer and sand to the topsoil. These simple measures will increase the soil's fertility and prevent excess water from accumulating.

Dahlia 'Orfeo' ▲

Family: *Compositae*
Height: 110 cm (43 in)

This majestic "semi-cactus" dahlia makes an excellent cut flower, not only because of its height but also its sober, uniformly purplish red color. Dahlias that are destined to be used as cut flowers need only a small corner of the garden. To increase the life of dahlias as cut flowers and to enjoy their full beauty, harvest them when the flower has fully opened; the stem of a mature flower is able to drink more water.

The corner of the garden dedicated to "cutting dahlias" must be exposed to full sun; this will encourage growth and the abundant production of flowers.

Dahlia 'Pablo' ▶

Family: *Compositae*
Height: 30 cm (12 in)

'Pablo' (or 'Pablo Gallery') is a dahlia of modest dimensions, often shorter than 30 cm (12 in) tall. This fact, along with its cheerful yellow flowers with pinkish red edges, makes it a perfect choice for growing indoors.

Dahlia 'Peter' ▼

Family: *Compositae*
Height: 110 cm (43 in)

This pink "decorative" dahlia is very similar to 'Franz Kafka,' both in the color and shape of its flowers, and its blooming period (July–October). 'Peter,' however, is a much taller dahlia.

Dahlia 'Procyon' ◄
Family: *Compositae*
Height: 110 cm (43 in)

This dahlia has vivid, double, flame-colored (yellow, orange and red) flowers, and is usually more than 1 m (3¼ ft) tall. The first experiments in hybridization were conducted two centuries ago, during the Napoleonic era, in an attempt to create taller plants with larger flowers and more petals than the original species. Dahlias were popular in Europe long before they became known as dahlias; they were first known in Europe by their Mexican name "acocitli."

Dahlia ► 'Purple Gem'
Family: *Compositae*
Height: 100 cm (39 in)

This typical "cactus" dahlia has fully double purple flowers with long, tightly rolled, tubular petals. If tubers are purchased from a garden center or by mail order, they should be packed in peat or sawdust; these materials protect the tubers from bruising and from becoming dehydrated. The tubers should be removed from their packing immediately prior to planting.

Dahlia

Dahlia ◄
'Red Pygmy'
Family: *Compositae*
Height: 50 cm (20 in)

Red is one of the most common colors of dahlias, and 'Red Pygmy' is another dahlia that is prized for its intense scarlet blooms. For an eye-catching display, these flashy dahlias can be planted with other types of flowering bulbs in the same color range, such as *Lilium* or flowering herbaceous plants like *Verbena*. To make these brightly colored dahlias stand out even more, plant them with *Cosmos*, *Eustoma* or the delicate pink *Lavatera*.

Dahlia 'Rosella' ◄
Family: *Compositae*
Height: 120 cm (47 in)

This "decorative" dahlia boasts deep pink flowers and is one of the tallest of all. Because of its large size, its tubers should be planted at least 40–50 cm (16–20 in) apart, but like most dahlias, can still be planted 10 cm (4 in) deep.

Dahlia 'Seattle' ▶

Family: *Compositae*
Height: 80 cm (31 in)

This variety offers a unique color combination: the central and basal portions of the flower are various shades of yellow while the tip of each petal is milky white.

Dahlias can be propagated in the spring by dividing their tuberous roots. It is a delicate operation that must be performed with a well-sharpened knife, making sure that each piece is connected to one piece of stem, at the base of which the new plants will sprout.

Dahlia 'Sneezy' ◀

Family: *Compositae*
Height: 40 cm (16 in)

'Sneezy,' a typical "mignon" dahlia, is a favorite of dahlia lovers. These dwarfish dahlias are 30–50 cm (12–20 in) tall and produce open, single flowers with a tight yellow inflorescence at their center. Although this particular cultivar has white blooms, there are yellow, pink and red varieties as well.

Dahlias are generally very easy to plant and "mignon" dahlias in pots or containers are great for the dahlia novice. Short-stemmed "topmix" dahlias produce many flowers and are also good beginner dahlias.

Dahlia

Dahlia 'Toto' ◄
Family: *Compositae*
Height: 40 cm (16 in)

"Anemone" dahlias are easy to recognize because of their uniquely shaped flowers. Each bloom is comprised of many small, tubular petals at its center, surrounded by one or two rings of longer outer petals. 'Toto' has light yellow center petals and white or silvery gray outer petals.

"Anemone" dahlias thrive both in containers and in the garden and can even be planted in a corner of a vegetable garden, perhaps mixed in with the green lettuce and red tomatoes.

Dahlia 'Tsuki ► Yori No Shisha'
Family: *Compositae*
Height: 90 cm (35 in)

'Tsuki Yori No Shisha' is a beautiful white "cactus" dahlia with a light yellow center.

When extracting tubers from the soil in the fall, do not forget to wipe them free of loose soil with a dry cloth and let them air-dry for a few days. Any damaged or rotten parts of the tuber should be removed with a sharp knife; the cut area should then be disinfected with a fungicidal powder.

Dahlia ▲ 'Vuurvogel'
Family: *Compositae*
Height: 100 cm (39 in)

With the tall and imposing 'Vuurvogel' in your garden, you scarcely need to plant any other flowers! Its vivid red-and-yellow flame-colored blooms and light and voluminous foliage, growing the length of its stems, make combinations with other plants almost superfluous. However, if your dahlias must have company, there are ways to solve this "problem." "Topmix" and other small "decorative" dahlias, for example, make nice a border edging, especially among perennials with ample rust-colored foliage. Also, the larger dahlias can be planted against a backdrop of like or contrasting colored roses.

Dahlia ▼ 'White Perfection'
Family: *Compositae*
Height: 120 cm (47 in)

'White Perfection,' a dahlia of considerable size, is well over 1 m (3¼ ft) tall. Its pure snow

white blooms stand out from the other white dahlias and are highly valued as cut flowers. Like the other dahlias described in this section, this dahlia can bloom for months.

Dahlia ▼ 'White Star'
Family: *Compositae*
Height: 110 cm (43 in)

'White Star' is another large dahlia with white flowers but, unlike 'White Perfection,' this variety is a "cactus" dahlia with flowers that are ivory, rather than pure white.

Dahlia 'Wittem' ◄

Family: *Compositae*
Height: 55 cm (22 in)

Although not very tall for a dahlia, 'Wittem' is appreciated for its white blooms with yellow-tinted centers and pink outer edges.

In colder or mountainous regions, dahlias can be kept on schedule by planting them indoors five or six weeks prior to the last frost date. Once transplanted into the garden, they will grow very rapidly.

Dahlia ► 'Yellow Star'

Family: *Compositae*
Height: 120 cm (47 in)

This "semi-cactus" dahlia owes its name to its luminous yellow bloom more than 1 m (3¼ ft) above the ground. Like all dahlias, 'Yellow Star' requires full sun, and the more light it gets each day, the more beautiful its flowers will be. If planted in a partially shaded corner of the garden or on the shady side of a patio, the stems will grow longer than normal and the flowers will look stunted.

Eucharis

*This genus of Amarylli-
daceae includes many
species native to South
America. Eucharis are not
easy to grow outdoors in
North America or in Europe
and usually must be grown
either in a greenhouse or
in containers that can be
brought outdoors during the
summer, and indoors, to a
heated location, during the
winter.*

Eucharis
amazonica
Family: Amaryllidaceae
Height: 60 cm (24 in)

Amazon lilies have umbels
composed of three to six delicately fragrant, white flowers
per stem, surrounded by lush,
green, ovate leaves. It naturally
blooms during the winter, but
it can be forced to bloom in
any season of the year; it is
usually forced to bloom in the
summer. In most climates it
must be grown indoors in a
sunny location (or in a greenhouse), away from the direct
rays of the sun. It must also
be kept relatively warm year-
round.

Bulbs should be planted in
a loam of leaves and sand
mixed with peat. Fertilize
with bonemeal or another
natural calcareous substance
and well-rotted manure.

Eucomis

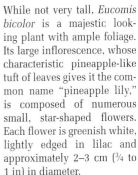

Eucomis are originally from South Africa (Cape Provinces), where they naturally bloom from mid to late summer, but they can also be grown in North America and Europe. Eucomis produce a few large basal leaves, sometimes over 50 cm (20 in) wide, and a robust flower stalk with numerous star-shaped flowers.

Eucomis ◄ autumnalis
Family: *Liliaceae*
Height: 30 cm (12 in)

Although this species is hardier than *Eucomis bicolor* it is much less prevalent. *E. autumnalis* has long bright green leaves with highly visible central veins and undulating edges. Its white-green flowers are very similar to those of *E. bicolor.*

Eucomis bicolor ◄
Family: *Liliaceae*
Height: 50 cm (20 in)

While not very tall, *Eucomis bicolor* is a majestic looking plant with ample foliage. Its large inflorescence, whose characteristic pineapple-like tuft of leaves gives it the common name "pineapple lily," is composed of numerous small, star-shaped flowers. Each flower is greenish white, lightly edged in lilac and approximately 2–3 cm (¾ to 1 in) in diameter.

    E. bicolor blooms from July to September and can survive outdoors only in mild climates and sheltered locations. Its bulbs are planted 15 cm (6 in) deep and 20–25 cm (8–10 in) apart in fertile, sandy, well-drained soil.

Freesia

*Freesias are members of
the family* Iridaceae *and
are originally from South
Africa. While there are
many naturally occurring
species of freesias, the summer blooming hybrids are
by far the most popular.
These hybrids have
lanceolate leaves and
multicolored, fragrant,
trumpet-shaped flowers.
Their stems are slender
and range from 30–45 cm
(12–18 in) in length.*

Freesia 'Single' ▶
Family: *Iridaceae*
Height: 40 cm (16 in)

These freesias are the traditional single variety and are
often sold in mixed color
assortments. Their corms are
planted 7–8 cm (2½–3 in)
deep and approximately 10
cm (4 in) apart. In colder
regions, try planting freesias
in containers, in a mixture of
sand, potting soil and peat.
Water abundantly and fertilize once a month during their
growing season. They bloom
between June and September
and must be brought indoors
during the winter.

Freesia 'Double' ◀
Family: *Iridaceae*
Height: 40 cm (16 in)

These freesias, often listed in
catalogs as "mixed doubles,"
are a mixed assortment of different colored double freesias,
in varying shades of yellow,
red, pink, orange, blue and
violet. In regions with temperate climates these plants
can be grown outdoors, as
long as they are planted in a
warm and sunny location;
however, they are generally
grown in containers.

Freesia

Galtonia
SUMMER HYACINTH

Galtonia candicans
Family: *Liliaceae*
Height: 100 cm (39 in)

Also known as the "summer hyacinth," *Galtonia candicans* has long, rigid stems that terminate in inflorescences composed of 20 to 30 delicately perfumed, bell-shaped flowers. Each flower is greenish white and 4 cm (1½ in) in length. Summer hyacinths are relatively hardy and bloom late in the summer, between August and September. Their bulbs are planted in April, 15 cm (6 in) deep and 15–20 cm (6–8 in) apart (for a compact grouping), in fertile, well-drained soil.

In colder regions, they can be forced in greenhouses for out of season blooming. In milder climates, bulbs can be left in the ground year-round as long they are protected by a winter mulch of dry leaves and the ground is not too damp. In more frigid climates, bulbs must be dug up and stored in a dry location for the winter. *Galtonia* can be propagated in the spring either by separating their bulbils or by planting their seeds in a greenhouse.

This member of the lily family is originally from southern Africa where it can be found growing all the way to the Cape of Good Hope in humid, grassy areas up to 2,500 m (8,200 ft) in elevation. Galtonia are generally rather tall and have long, thin, lanceolate leaves. Their numerous, sparsely distributed, bell-shaped flowers are relatively small considering the plant's size. Although Galtonia has many loyal fans, it is not nearly as popular as many other bulbs and only Galtonia candicans, with its delicately perfumed white bells, is commonly available. The bulbs of Galtonia are large and round.

Gladiolus

Gladiolus

Gladioli are Iridaceae *originally from the Mediterranean or subtropical regions. They have long, straight stems with spikes of irregular, funnel-shaped flowers of various sizes, shapes and colors, surrounded by thin, grasslike leaves. In the 1800s floriculturists began creating the hybrids that today have almost completely replaced the naturally occurring species.*

Gladiolus ▶ 'Amsterdam'
Family: *Iridaceae*
Height: 170 cm (67 in)

This lovely white gladiolus is a "large-flowering" variety. Each inflorescence is 70–80 cm (28–31 in) long and is comprised of 24 to 27 flowers, at least 10 of which are in bloom at once.

Gladiolus ◀ callianthus 'Murielae'
Family: *Iridaceae*
Height: 70 cm (28 in)

Although it is sometimes cataloged as *Acidanthera bicolor*, *Gladiolus callianthus* is a unique species of gladiolus native to the tropical regions of Africa. It has beautiful spikes of white flowers with irregular purple markings at their centers. 'Murielae' is the largest and most hardy variety.

Gladiolus ▼ 'Elvira'
Family: *Iridaceae*
Height: 50 cm (20 in)

Slightly more than 50 cm (20 in) tall, 'Elvira' is one of the smallest hybrids. Its smaller dimensions, however, make it particularly suitable for growing in pots. Its pale pink flowers with magenta cores are also valued cut flow-ers. Its corms are planted from March to April, 8 cm (3 in) deep and 10 cm (4 in) apart. It blooms from June to August.

Gladiolus ▲ colvillei 'Albus'
Family: *Iridaceae*
Height: 50 cm (20 in)

The South African *Gladiolus colvillei* is very similar to *Gladiolus nanus,* with which it is sometimes combined by some botanists. While not very tall for a gladiolus, it is hardier and blooms earlier (June–August) than other species. The variety 'Albus' produces a short spike of a few white flowers that are even more funnel-shaped than those of other gladioli.

Gladiolus

Gladiolus ▾ 'Fidelius'

Family: *Iridaceae*
Height: 100 cm (39 in)

'Fidelius' is one of the most popular hybrids. It produces many magenta flowers in mid-summer. Like most varieties in this genus, its corms are planted 10 cm (4 in) deep and 15 cm (6 in) apart.

Gladiolus ▴ 'Friendship'

Family: *Iridaceae*
Height: 100 cm (39 in)

'Friendship' is another typical hybrid, similar to 'Fidelius,' but with delicate reddish orange flowers. Like all bulbs, gladioli need nutrients, which must be administered at specific times during the growing season. Before planting, add an organic fertilizer that gradually releases nutrients into the soil, such as well-rotted manure. A balanced mineral fertilizer should also be applied as soon as the new growth pokes through the soil. When corms are properly fed, they will continue to bloom year after year.

Gladiolus ‣ 'Nova Lux'
Family: Iridaceae
Height: 90 cm (35 in)

"Lux" (or "light") undoubtedly makes reference to these gladiolis' luminous yellow flowers. 'Nova Lux' can be kept from rotting or developing mold by following a few easy guidelines. If your soil tends to be on the damp side, a handful of sand should be sprinkled into each bulb hole before planting. This will allow water to drain down into the soil and away from

Gladiolus ▲ 'Her Majesty'
Family: *Iridaceae*
Height: 100 cm (39 in)

This gladiolus has intense pinkish violet flowers that gradually fade to white towards their centers. Like other gladioli, 'Her Majesty' has small, round, turniplike corms that are slightly flattened at each end. A healthy corm should be firm to the touch and there should be no grayish green spots of mold growing on its surface.

Gladiolus ‣ 'Hunting Song'
Family: *Iridaceae*
Height: 90 cm (35 in)

'Hunting Song' is one of the many varieties of red gladioli, but can be distinguished from the other red varieties by its intense scarlet flowers. The bright-colored gladioli will brighten any border and can be planted next to bushes and herbaceous perennials with little difficulty. For example, the red gladiola can be used to bring out the silvery gray markings in the foliage of *Artemisia*.

the corm. Also, in the fall, before the first frost, corms should be removed from the soil and immediately dipped in fungicide and left to air dry before being stored in a cool, dry location for the winter.

Gladiolus ▶ 'Nymph'
Family: *Iridaceae*
Height: 60 cm (24 in)

'Nymph,' only 60 cm (24 in) tall, is a dwarf gladiolus. However, it's particularly appreciated for the beauty of its white flowers, which have elegant bright red diamonds on each petal.

Gladiolus

Gladiolus ▼ 'Plumtart'

Family: *Iridaceae*
Height: 90 cm (35 in)

This hybrid is highly valued for its sumptuous purple flowers, often used in cut-flower arrangements. Despite its large size, 'Plumtart' can be grown in containers as long as the container is deep enough to allow the corms to be covered with at least 10 cm (4 in) of soil and sand. After planting, containers must be placed in a sunny location and protected from any cold drafts.

Gladiolus ▲ 'Peter Pears'

Family: *Iridaceae*
Height: 100 cm (39 in)

'Peter Pears,' appreciated for its sober, yet luminous, melon-colored flowers, blooms from August to late September. Different varieties of gladioli have slightly different summer blooming periods so with careful planning, you can have gladioli in bloom for the entire summer. After the blooms have withered, the stems should be cut down to approximately 20 cm (8 in) and the remaining portion of the stem used to locate the corms. The corms must be extracted from the soil, wiped clean of excess soil and left to dry. The withered stem can then be cut all the way down. Use a fungicide to disinfect corms before storing them in a cool, dark location, preferably in a paper bag, for the winter.

Gladiolus 'Praga' ▼

Family: *Iridaceae*
Height: 100 cm (39 in)

'Praga' is yet another elegant gladiolus hybrid. The immense number of hybrids that exist today is not surprising since botanists and floriculturists have been developing new breeds since 1841. The majority of the 'Grandiflorus' hybrids, however, were not developed until a century later. Today there are many varieties that differ only in size, color or height (large, medium and dwarf).

Gladiolus ▲ 'Priscilla'

Family: *Iridaceae*
Height: 100 cm (39 in)

'Priscilla' has rich, cream-colored flowers with yellow throats and petals outlined in bright pink. After planting, corms must be watered generously and covered with a layer of mulch or wood chips. Fertilize the soil when the gladioli begin to form buds, and again when the flowers start to wither. In mild climates the corms can be left in the ground year-round. In colder climates, however, the corms must be removed from the soil after the flowers have withered, but before the first frost, and stored in a cool, dry spot.

Gladiolus ▼ 'Traderhorn'

Family: *Iridaceae*
Height: 100 cm (39 in)

'Traderhorn' has pleasing mandarin red blooms with a white stripe down the center of each tepal. The lowest flowers on the stem bloom before those located at end of the stem. When the topmost flowers are in bloom, the lowest flowers on the stem have already withered. Each stem is surrounded by thin, linear, light green leaves with a hint of silver or pale blue.

Gladiolus ▲ 'Victor Borge'

Family: *Iridaceae*
Height: 100 cm (39 in)

Like 'Traderhorn,' this hybrid also has red flowers with a white stripe down the middle of each tepal, but the flowers of 'Victor Borge' are more orange.

Required planting depth depends on the size of both the plant and the bulb itself. Corms are generally planted 10–12 cm (4–5 in) deep, with modest variations for the dwarf and giant gladioli. About 10–20 cm (4–8 in) should be left between each corm, depending on whether the gladioli are to appear loosely or tightly clustered together. In either case, gladioli should always be planted on a bed of sand mixed with organic fertilizer and covered with ordinary garden soil.

Gladiolus

Gladiolus ▼
'Wind Song'
Family: *Iridaceae*
Height: 100 cm (39 in)

Uncommon, lilac-colored flowers with creamy white throats evenly line the tall, straight stems of this cultivar. Like 'Wind Song,' many gladiolus hybrids are 100 cm (39 in) tall, but some *Gladiolus nanus* (dwarf) varieties reach only 45 cm (18 in) in height, and some "giant" varieties reach 2 m (6½ ft). Most hybrids produce only one flower spike per corm, but some dwarf hybrids produce two or three. Also, some stems are curved, while others are perfectly straight.

Gladiolus ▲
'White Prosperity'
Family: *Iridaceae*
Height: 100 cm (39 in)

'White Prosperity' is a hybrid with innocent white blooms that are slightly darker at their throats. This eternal classic holds its own next to the new, brightly colored hybrids, which range from dusky orange or copper to violet, plum, lilac or blue.

Gloriosa
CLIMBING LILY

Gloriosa superba 'Rothschildiana'
Family: *Liliaceae*
Height: 150 cm (59 in)

This climbing lily has large, smooth, white tubers that are very fragile and covered by dry, brown and flaky tunics. Its slender stems sometimes reach 2 m (79 in) in height. Long, thin tendrils, located at the tip of each lanceolate leaf, are what the plant uses to attach itself to its climbing supports (which should be provided). Its backward arching scarlet flowers, outlined in bright, contrasting yellow, are very ornate and almost futuristic-looking with their long slender tepals. Each flower is 8–10 cm (3–4 in) in diameter.

'Rothschildiana' is a delicate climbing lily that blooms from July to September, and can only be overwintered outdoors in the mildest of climates. Its tubers are planted in containers in the spring and kept at 16–18°C (61–64°F) in a mixture of soil, sand and peat and a small amount of manure. Water generously and fertilize every two weeks during its growing season until it blooms. Keep 'Rothschildiana' out of the direct sun during the summer months.

The tall flowering vines of the Gloriosa *genus are unusual among flowering bulbs. Originally from tropical Africa, this member of the lily family has more than one species, but only* Gloriosa superba *cultivars, like 'Carsonii,' 'Lutea' and 'Rothschildiana' (considered to be the most spectacular variety) are commonly grown. Gloriosas can be propagated by dividing their tubers in the spring or by planting seeds. However, seeds will not produce flowers for four years. In the fall, when their leaves begin to dry and wither, tubers must be carefully extracted from the soil and stored in a cool, dry location until the spring.*

Gloriosa

Hymenocallis
Spider Lily

This genus of Amaryllidaceae *includes many tropical species, like* Hymenocallis narcissiflora *and* Hymenocallis longipetala, *characterized by their large bulbs, long, linear leaves and 40–70 cm (16–28 in) stems, depending on species. Spider lilies have very distinct, trumpetshaped, fragrant white flowers.*

Hymenocallis ▲ 'Advance'
Family: *Amaryllidaceae*
Height: 60 cm (24 in)

Native to Peru, *Hymenocallis narcissiflora* is the most popular species in its genus. It was first brought to Europe in the late 1700s and cultivated on a large scale for the cut-flower market. 'Advance' is 50–70 cm (20–28 in) tall and offers fragrant clusters of five large flowers that are generally 15 cm (6 in) in diameter. It produces white, trumpet-shaped flowers with long, thin, backward arching petals from July to August and is very sensitive to the cold. 'Advance' can only survive outdoors in very warm and sunny tropical climates and, therefore, is generally grown indoors. Its bulbs are planted 10 cm (4 in) deep and 20 cm (8 in) apart in permeable, humusrich soil (or in containers, in an equal mix of potting soil, peat and sand).

Hymenocallis ▼ 'Sulfur Queen'
Family: *Amaryllidaceae*
Height: 40 cm (16 in)

'Sulfur Queen' is similar to 'Advance' and should be watered generously and fertilized every two weeks until it blooms. It can be propagated by dividing its bulbils.

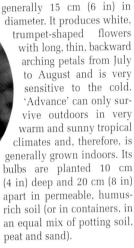

205

Hymenocallis

Incarvillea

The plants in this genus are originally from Central Asia (Tibet, Nepal and Western China), but have also adapted well to other regions. Although often confused with gloxinia, Incarvillea is a separate genus belonging to the family Bignoniaceae, another member of the wide world of bulbs.

Incarvillea delavayi

Family: *Bignoniaceae*
Height: 45 cm (18 in)

This perennial species has tuberous roots, which should be planted only 5 cm (2 in) deep and 20 cm (8 in) apart, in moist, well-drained soil, in a warm, sunny location. *Incarvillea delavayi* blooms in early to mid-summer. A thick stalk rising from a roselike bed of basal leaves supports several splendid, pink, trumpet-shaped flowers with yellow throats.

Liatris

Liatris spicata ◄
Family: *Compositae*
Height: 70 cm (28 in)

Liatris spicata is native to North America but also grows well in Europe, especially in the cooler regions. It has long tufts of grasslike leaves and a densely packed spike of numerous tiny flowers in varying tones of pink, magenta and white. Its corms are planted 5 cm (2 in) deep and 10 cm (4 in) apart.

Liatris are generally 70–80 cm (28–31 in) tall. They have long, cylindrical, brushlike inflorescences that bloom from top to bottom, and can resemble ornamental onions.

Liatris spicata ►
'Alba'
Family: *Compositae*
Height: 75 cm (30 in)

The variety 'Alba' has white flowers and is only slightly taller than the original species. It grows well in pots and is an excellent cut flower. 'Alba' blooms in July–August, beginning with the flowers located at the top of each inflorescence. It prefers full or partial sun.

Liatris

Lilium
LILY

Lilium 'Acapulco'
Family: *Liliaceae*
Height: 80 cm (31 in)

'Acapulco' is characterized by delicate pink blooms with dark pink freckles and stripes on each tepal. Its yellow and orange reproductive organs are, like those of all lilies, comprised of six stamens and a pistil with a three-lobed stigma. As with the other lilies, its bulbs are planted approximately 15 cm (6 in) deep and 30–45 cm (12–18 in) apart in groups of three or four.

Lilies are considered by many to be the most beautiful and popular of all the flowering bulbs. They are ideal for adding an accent of color to borders of herbaceous perennials, adding depth to evergreen hedges, or accompanying small shrubs. They also do well in containers and will brighten any balcony or patio. There are approximately 100 species in the Lilium genus, but the countless cultivars are more commercially available. Single flowers or racemes bloom atop tall, straight stems. Its flowers are comprised of six petals (or more accurately, tepals) and run the gamut of colors from white to red, passing through the various tonalities of yellow and orange. Although lilies come in many colors, the violet tones are completely absent. Its leaves can be elliptical, oval or bladelike, and light or dark green. In the wild, lilies are found only in the temperate zones of the Northern Hemisphere, between the 11th and 68th parallels, in regions with alternating hot and cold seasons or periods of rain and drought. Contrary to popular belief, lilies can be grown fairly easily by even the least experienced gardener, with the help of a few small tricks.

Lilium ▲ 'Avignon'

Family: *Liliaceae*
Height: 70 cm (28 in)

'Avignon' has bright orange flowers, with red reflections at the tip of each tepal and dark red-tipped stamens. Like most lilies, 'Avignon' makes an excellent cut flower, but keep in mind that if the plant is deprived of almost all of its leaves when its flowers are cut, it will not be able to perform photosynthesis and may die from lack of nutrients. Lilies also need well-drained soil; excess humidity can cause them to rot and prevents the bud (the new stem)

from growing. This problem can be easily avoided by sprinkling a few handfuls of sand in each bulb hole before planting.

Lilium ▶ 'Barbaresco'

Family: *Liliaceae*
Height: 80 cm (31 in)

This lily has one of the highest color contrasts between the heart of the flower and the outer portion of its petals. 'Barbaresco' has dark magenta petals with the usual sprinkling of darker freckles, but its heart is yellow and green with a light outline that makes it stand out from the rest of

the flower. Like all lily hybrids, 'Barbaresco' blooms all summer, from around the beginning of June to the end of August. It is also pleasantly perfumed, a quality that not all lilies share.

Lilium 'Berlin' ▶

Family: *Liliaceae*
Height: 75 cm (30 in)

While this cultivar is usually 70–80 cm (28–31 in) tall, it is not one of the taller members of the *Lilium* family; the tallest lilies can reach 120 cm (47 in) in height. 'Berlin' has elegant pink blooms with darker red stripes and a sprinkling of darker freckles. Its heart is bright yellow and green with ivory green filaments supporting dark purple anthers. Even one or two 'Berlin' lilies planted next to evergreen hedges will give them depth and make them stand out. This technique

Lilium

Lilium ▾ 'Casa Blanca'

Family: *Liliaceae*
Height: 90 cm (35 in)

This striking lily is characterized by its pure white flower. While 'Casa Blanca' is not the only white lily, it is one of the very few. The white lily has always had symbolic significance and is one of the most recurring symbols in Italian paintings of the 13th and 14th centuries, and Dutch paintings of the 15th century. The most famous of these works is probably the triptych by Botticelli, in which the Virgin is surrounded by eight angels, each holding a white lily. In Greek and Roman times the white lily was a symbol of divinity.

works well both in a more geometric formal garden and in the simple perimeter hedge of a country garden. This lily also has a rich perfume.

tracted from the soil, cleaned and stored in a box of wood chips or sand, which must be kept moist through the winter. To maintain sufficient moisture, lightly spray with water every two weeks.

Lilium ▼
'Connecticut King'
Family: *Liliaceae*
Height: 70 cm (28 in)

This hybrid has a bright yellow bloom with a green throat and contrasting brown anthers. Although there are some lilies that can tolerate the partial shade of the woodland underbrush, 'Connecticut King,' like most lilies, prefers full sun. Generally speaking, lilies with brightly colored flowers require more sun, whereas those with white or lightly colored flowers prefer partial sun.

Lilium ▲
'Con Amore'
Family: *Liliaceae*
Height: 80 cm (31 in)

The high contrast between its classic powdery pink petals and bright red anthers makes this lily unique. Like other hybrids, 'Con Amore' is relatively hardy. In the fall, in regions where the average temperature does not dip below 10°C (50°F), its stems can be cut and bulbs can left in the ground year-round, as long as they are covered with a winter mulch. In colder regions, bulbs must be ex-

Lilium

Lilium 'Donau' ◄

Family: *Liliaceae*
Height: 60 cm (24 in)

Although lilies are generally not thought of as house-plants, they can be easily grown in almost any kind of container, as long as it is big enough and the general planting requirements are adhered to. The modest height of this cream-colored hybrid, with characteristic dark speckles and stripes, makes it particularly well suited to growing in pots.

Lilium 'Le Rêve' ◄

Family: *Liliaceae*
Height: 70 cm (28 in)

'Le Rêve' is another lily of uncommon beauty. Its delicate pink tepals are pleasantly accented with a sprinkling of tiny red freckles and dark central veins. The intricate coloration found in its lemon yellow and green center and dark ocher throat and anthers is almost a flower within a flower.

Not surprisingly, this sweet-smelling lily is very popular, both in the garden and as a cut flower.

Lilium ▶ 'Méditerranée'

Family: *Liliaceae*
Height: 75 cm (30 in)

The two shades of pink found in 'Méditerranée' are harmoniously brought together in an ideal balance of colors. Plant this dazzling pink Oriental hybrid with other pink flowers to create a "romantic" corner in your garden. Some suitable pink companion flowers include hydrangea, snapdragons, double daisies and mignon dahlias. If there is no room left in your garden for lilies, don't worry, lilies also grow well in pots and can be placed among the shrubs and perennials or in any spot that needs beautifying.

Lilium ◀ 'Mona Lisa'

Family: *Liliaceae*
Height: 40 cm (16 in)

Like 'Casa Blanca' and 'Star Gazer,' 'Mona Lisa' is an Oriental hybrid. These hybrids are all cultivars of Asian (particularly Japanese) species, like *Lilium auratum, Lilium japonicum* and *Lilium speciosum,* which are all highly valued for their beauty. Oriental hybrids generally have very fragrant flowers and bloom in a vast array of colors.

Lilium ▶ 'Moneymaker'

Family: *Liliaceae*
Height: 75 cm (30 in)

'Moneymaker' is another pink hybrid, but is more uniform in color than other varieties. The usual planting requirements apply: 15 cm (6 in) deep and at least 25 cm (10 in) apart.

Lilium ◀ 'Monte Negro'

Family: *Liliaceae*
Height: 80 cm (31 in)

'Monte Negro' is a beautiful lily with reddish orange flowers. Its bulbs must be planted as soon after they have been purchased as possible, otherwise the bulb scales may become dehydrated. As always, bulb holes should be twice the height of the bulb and a handful of sand should be sprinkled at the bottom of each hole to increase drainage. Lilies can tolerate alkaline soil, but if this is the case, they should be fertilized with well-rotted manure.

Lilium 'Navona' ▾
Family: *Liliaceae*
Height: 60 cm (24 in)

The uniformity of this hybrid's snow white petals is interrupted only by hints of yellow and green at its throat and the dark brown of its anthers. There are many great ways to use this extraordinary lily in your garden. For example, white or light flowered varieties, like 'Navona,' grow

Lilium 'Muscadet' ▴
Family: *Liliaceae*
Height: 60 cm (24 in)

'Muscadet' has a lovely white bloom with pink "leopard spots" and bright orange anthers. Like all lilies, with a little patience and care, it can be propagated and spread with even a very limited number of bulbs. In fact, after a few years of consistent blooming, if the bulb is healthy, it will spontaneously produce new bulbs.

To propagate, carefully detach the scales from the mother bulb and place them in containers filled with a mixture of potting soil and sand. Do not bury the scales in the soil, but rather insert them so that they are standing upright and only the "root" is covered with about 1 cm (½ in) of soil. Place the container in a warm and sunny location and spray frequently with a fine mist of water. The scales grow slowly, but don't get discouraged; new lilies will eventually begin to appear.

Lilium

excellently in the partially shady corners of a large garden surrounded by a downy carpet of ferns. A humid climate and slightly acidic soil are ideal growing conditions for lilies. The rays of the morning or afternoon sun will encourage the blooms to open, while the partial shade from the hot afternoon sun will make them last longer.

Lilium 'Romano' ▲
Family: *Liliaceae*
Height: 80 cm (31 in)

The sunny yellow flowers of this beautiful lily make it easy to pair with other flowers. Petunias and *Tagetes*, for example, are splendid summer bloomers that grow happily in full sun and, like lilies, do not mind restricted spaces. They also have similar climatic and growth requirements as lilies, making them good companion plants. For a dazzling display, combine 'Romano' (or other yellow or white lilies) with white petunias and large, golden, double *Tagetes erecta*.

Lilium ◄ 'Royal Fantasy'
Family: *Liliaceae*
Height: 80 cm (31 in)

'Royal Fantasy' offers delicate yellow-and-white blooms with pale green veins that are also visible on the outside of the tepals.

Like all lilies, if given the proper conditions will grow just about anywhere. For example, shrubs can be used to shelter lilies from dominant winds; rosemary bushes grow well in warmer gardens, while asparagus ferns can be used in cooler climates and partial shade.

Lilium 'Simplon' ►
Family: *Liliaceae*
Height: 90 cm (35 in)

Six crimson anthers perched atop delicate green filaments and accompanied by a conspicuous green pistil make this tall and slender white lily easy to tell apart from the other white lilies.

Lilium 'Snow Queen'

Family: *Liliaceae*
Height: 80 cm (31 in)

It is difficult to know whether 'Snow Queen' is a pink or a white lily, so delicate is the balance between the two shades. However, the general color range of a lily as well as its size can be determined by simply looking at its bulb. If the bulb scales are distinctly white then its flower will be white, and if they are slightly reddish or dark pink, its flower will be red or pink.

Lily bulbs are generally about the size of a fist; smaller bulbs generally produce smaller plants and larger bulbs produce larger plants. The bulb scales of this pleasantly fragrant hybrid are usually milky white and sometimes slightly yellow.

Lilium

Lilium 'Star Gazer'

Family: *Liliaceae*
Height: 70 cm (28 in)

This Oriental hybrid, well known for its delicate perfume and rich color, is one of the most popular lilies. Like other lilies, 'Star Gazer' blooms in mid-summer and can only be left in the ground year-round in regions where the winter temperature does not dip below 10°C (50°F). Even in mild climates, bulbs should be protected from unexpected cold weather by a winter mulch of leaves and manure.

Lilium 'Tiara' ◄
Family: *Liliaceae*
Height: 80 cm (31 in)

This lily's delicate pink blooms, bleached with white, are considered to be some of the most beautiful among the pink lilies.

As with all lilies, whenever possible, be sure to check the condition of the bulbs before purchasing; the bulb scales should not be broken or damaged in any way, nor should there be any green spots, which are a probable indication of a fungal disease. Bulbs should always be packed in wood chips to avoid dehydration. If you cannot plant your bulbs immediately, store them in a wooden or cardboard box and cover them with a layer of sand mixed with moist peat. However, it is always a good idea to plant bulbs as soon as possible.

Lilium tigrinum ◄
Family: *Liliaceae*
Height: 90 cm (35 in)

Although the market is dominated by countless lily hybrids, some botanical species are still available. The tiger lily (*Lilium tigrinum*), for example, is a popular botanical species, originally from East Asia where it has been cultivated for centuries for its edible bulbs. Tiger lilies prefer non-alkaline soil and full sun.

221

Lilium

Lilium 'Vivaldi' ▾
Family: *Liliaceae*
Height: 75 cm (30 in)

'Vivaldi' is another beautiful variety of lily with uniformly pink flowers, interrupted only by a light sprinkling of tiny dark freckles. Like other lily hybrids, it blooms in the summer (July–August) and is easy to grow, as long as its

Lilium 'Uchida' ▴
Family: *Liliaceae*
Height: 80 cm (31 in)

This lovely tiger lily hybrid with white, pink and red petals is a favorite around the globe. Lilies are popular in Asia, especially Japan, as well as in Europe and North America. The magnificently colored Oriental hybrids, with their inebriating perfume, have been derived from East Asian species. In the United States, many Oriental hybrids have been bred for larger blooms and more flowers per stem, but this has compromised their fragrance.

Lilium

bulbs are planted 15 cm (6 in) deep and 25–30 cm (10–12 in) apart. 'Vivaldi' also makes an excellent cut flower.

Lilium 'Woodriff's ▸ Memory'

Family: *Liliaceae*
Height: 80 cm (31 in)

Last, but not least, 'Woodriff's Memory' offers a glorious

blend of pink and yellow blooms. Its salmon pink petals gradually lighten towards their centers, where touches of yellow and bright orange highlight the throat and stamens. The wide array of colors found in the *Lilium* genus make them easy to combine with other flowers, and the possible combinations with perennials in mixed borders, beds and along garden paths are endless. However, the warmer colored lilies pair beautifully with blue, lilac and pink flowers, like *Salvia nemorosa*, *Aster amellus* and *Veronica longifolia*. White and light pink lilies, on the other hand, combine well with *Lavandula stoechas*, and the darker pink lilies can be paired with snapdragons and *Achillea* in the same color range. The vivacious beauty of all lilies can be accentuated by combining them with silver-leafed herbaceous plants, like *Stachys byzantina*, *Hosta sieboldiana glauca* or any in the genus *Artemisia*.

Mirabilis
Four-o'clock

The **Nyctaginaceae** *are present in the world of flowering bulbs thanks to the genus* **Mirabilis.** **Mirabilis,** *or "four-o'clock," unlike other bulbs, are bushy, 60–70 cm (24–28 in) in height, dotted with numerous multicolored flowers.*

Mirabilis jalapa
Family: *Nyctaginaceae*
Height: 60 cm (24 in)

The bulbs of *Mirabilis jalapa* are planted 15 cm (6 in) deep and 25 cm (10 in) apart, preferably in full sun, although in warmer regions they will tolerate partial shade. Their fragrant, trumpet-shaped flowers bloom from mid-summer to early fall, in an array of colors including white, yellow, pink, orange and red.

Nerine
Guernsey Lily

The South African Guernsey lily belongs to the family **Amaryllidaceae.** *Its beauty and long shelf life as a cut flower have made* **Nerine** *very popular in Europe and North America. Although* **Nerine bowdenii** *is not particularly hardy, its lovely flowers have made it a favorite. It blooms from late summer to early fall.*

Nerine bowdenii
Family: *Amaryllidaceae*
Height: 45 cm (18 in)

Guernsey lilies have long, thin, dark green leaves, and a rigid stem topped by an umbel of eight to 12 trumpetlike flowers, with sinuous, undulating petals. Its flowers are pale pink with a darker central vein.

Guernsey lilies are sensitive to winter frost and can survive outdoors through the winter only in warmer regions and in sunny locations. In more frigid climates they can be grown as annuals or indoors in containers.

Ornithogalum
STAR OF BETHLEHEM

SUMMER BULBS

Ornithogalum arabicum

Family: *Liliaceae*
Height: 50 cm (20 in)

This Mediterranean species grows naturally along the rocky coasts of the Mediterranean basin. The average height listed above is strictly a rough estimate, as its height commonly ranges from 30–100 cm (12–39 in). *Ornithogalum arabicum* is rather delicate and should be planted in a sheltered location. Its bulbs are planted 7–8 cm (2½–3 in) deep, and not more than 15 cm (6 in) apart to obtain a dense grouping. Its stems support crowded inflorescences comprised of numerous tiny, white, star-shaped flowers with black ovaries. The soil should be fertile and free-draining. *O. arabicum* blooms in early summer.

Ornithogalum, *or star of Bethlehem, is a member of the family* Liliaceae. *The species in this genus differ tremendously from one another both in height and in the color of their flowers. Some ornithogalums are only about 20 cm (8 in) tall, while others can reach more than 1 m (3¼ ft). Their flowers are usually white, but can also be yellow or* orange, depending on the species. These differences are easily understandable when their origins are taken into consideration. Some species are native to South Africa, while others are native to western Asia and Europe. This also explains their disparate growth requirements, blooming seasons (the spring bloomers are illustrated in the pre- *vious section) and hardiness; some members of this genus are extremely hardy while others are extremely delicate.*

Ornithogalum

Ornithogalum ▼ saundersiae
Family: *Liliaceae*
Height: 100 cm (39 in)

This species offers compact, spherical, tree-like umbels comprised of numerous white, star-shaped flowers with black and yellow reproductive organs. Each flower cluster is perched atop a long, slender stem that is sometimes more than 1 m (3¼ ft) tall.

Ornithogalum ▲ dubium
Family: *Liliaceae*
Height: 20 cm (8 in)

Ornithogalum dubium is the smallest *Ornithogalum* presented in this survey, but it is a very popular variety that grows well in containers and is easily forced. Its small bulbs are planted 5 cm (2 in) deep and 7–8 cm (2½–3 in) apart. Its short stem is topped by a cluster of small, glowing orange flowers and surrounded by dark green basal leaves. *O. dubium* blooms throughout the summer (July–September) and makes an excellent cut flower, especially when used in mixed flower bouquets.

Its bulbs should not be planted more than 5 cm (2 in) deep and 20 cm (8 in) apart. *Ornithogalum saundersiae* blooms throughout the summer (July–September) and is a highly valued cut flower.

227

Ornithogalum ▲ thyrsoides
Family: *Liliaceae*
Height: 40 cm (16 in)

This variety of *Ornithogalum* has fleshy green leaves that are 25–30 cm (10–12 in) long. Its flowers, collected in dense clusters, are white and star-shaped with long, orange stamens and brown ovaries. *O. thyrsoides* is not a very hardy species and can only be over-wintered outdoors in very warm climates. In colder climates, bulbs can be grown as annuals or planted in containers filled with a mix of soil, peat and sand. Its bulbs are planted in the spring, 7–8 cm (2½–3 in) deep, in a warm and sunny location, in fertile, well-drained soil.

It can be propagated by separating its bulbils, or by planting its seeds. The seeds, however, take four years to start producing flowers. It blooms from July to September.

Ornithogalum

Oxalis

60

Oxalis ◄ adenophylla

Family: *Oxalidaceae*
Height: 10 cm (4 in)

This delicate looking, dwarfish plant is originally from Chile and blooms from late spring to early summer. Its grayish green leaves are 5–10 cm (2–4 in) long and composed of numerous leaflets and scapes. When in bloom, *Oxalis adenophylla* becomes an attractive cushion of funnel-shaped flowers. Each flower is 3 cm (1 in) in diameter and has five white-and-lilac petals.

The family Oxalidaceae *includes both spring and summer-blooming species. The South African* Oxalis cernua *(described in the previous section) produces splendid yellow flowers and is a spring-blooming species, while* Oxalis adenophylla, Oxalis deppei *and* Oxalis enneaphylla *are all summer–fall blooming varieties. The family* Oxalidaceae *is unique because it includes rhizomes, tubers and tuberous roots that are often uncommon in shape and appearance.*

228

Oxalis

It is a hardy species, ideal for rock gardens, and its peculiar bulbs, resembling balls of felt, can be planted in the fall or spring 10 cm (4 in) deep and the same distance apart. It can be propagated by separating its rhizomes towards the end of the summer. It will grow happily in a sunny location with well-drained, fertile soil that has been amended with peat and sand. *O. adenophylla* should be fertilized at the beginning of the growth season and can survive outdoors year-round with no further care. It can also be grown in flowerpots filled with ordinary potting soil.

Oxalis deppei ◄ 'Iron Cross'
Family: *Oxalidaceae*
Height: 15 cm (6 in)

Oxalis deppei or *Oxalis tetraphylla*, like other oxalis, is a dwarf species that does not always reach a full 15 cm (6 in) in height. *O. deppei* is originally from Mexico, but its cultivar has since become popular in other parts of North America as well as in Europe, where it is commonly grown in containers or gardens.

It has a taproot covered with proliferous bulbils, and leaves comprised of four heart-shaped leaflets. 'Iron Cross' has delicate red flowers with dark green, yellow and white centers.

Oxalis ▲ enneaphylla
Family: *Oxalidaceae*
Height: 10 cm (4 in)

This species is native to the Falkland Islands and the cooler regions of southern Chile where it grows naturally in the sandy soil along the coast. *Oxalis enneaphylla* is very similar to (and often confused with) *Oxalis adeno-phylla*, but it has longer tuberous roots, two to three flower stems per plant and its leaves are less deeply cleft. Light pink stripes run longitudinally down each magenta petal, which gradually fade to white towards the center of the flower. Its bright yellow stamens contrast with its dark purple throat.

Oxalis regnellii ▼

Family: *Oxalidaceae*
Height: 15 cm (6 in)

This species of oxalis has snow white flowers and, like the other members of its genus, is rather small in size, usually only about 15 cm (6 in) or less in height. Despite its size, it is very popular with gardeners because it is easy to grow and requires little space. Its small bulbs are planted just 3 cm (1 in) deep and not more than 5 cm (2 in) apart. *Oxalis regnellii* are perfect for growing in flowerpots, window boxes or any other type of container that strikes your fancy. They may look delicate, but oxalis are actually very hardy, a quality that only contributes to their popularity. In climates where the winters are not too cold, they can easily be grown outdoors in full or partial sun and rich soil.

Oxalis triangularis ▶

Family: *Oxalidaceae*
Height: 20 cm (8 in)

Oxalis triangularis is slightly taller, but is otherwise very similar to other types of oxalis. It can be distinguished from the other varieties by the signature color of its leaves and flowers. Its powdery pink blooms, when planted in large groups, cover the ground in charming pink clouds. Its leaves are also unique in that

the common green color has been replaced with shades of gray and violet. Like other varieties, however, *O. triangularis* blooms all summer and grows well both in containers and in the garden, climate permitting. Its bulbs are planted close together and near the surface and will come back year after year as long they are covered with a winter mulch to keep the bulbs from freezing. This species is also easy to propagate by the division of its bulbils.

Pleione

This genus is native to Taiwan and Tibet. It is a member of the orchid family and includes the splendid terrestrial orchids with

pseudobulbs. Pleione can be propagated during repotting by separating the buds that form at the base of its pseudobulbs.

Pleione formosana
Family: *Orchidaceae*
Height: 15 cm (6 in)

Pleione formosana has 2–3-cm (½–1-in) long pseudobulbs, and leaves that often do not appear until after the flower has bloomed. Its stems are 10–15 cm (4–6 in) long and support extraordinary white to purple flowers. Its flowers can have a maximum diameter of 10 cm (4 in). Their natural blooming season is spring, but they are generally forced to bloom in mid-summer (July–August).

In mild climates, they can be grown outdoors in sheltered locations, partial shade and light, well-drained soil that has been enriched with leaves and peat. In containers, they can be planted in two parts potting soil and one part sphagnum moss.

Polianthes
TUBEROSE

The Mexican genus Polianthes includes Polianthes tuberosa, commonly called the "tuberose." Tuberoses have unusual rhizomes on which bulbs grow surrounded by smaller bulbils. The tuberose has a straight stem, long, thin leaves and spikes of very fragrant, tube-shaped, white flowers that open like a star. It blooms from mid-summer to early fall and can be propagated by separating its newly formed tubers, which should then be transferred to a greenhouse.

Polianthes tuberosa 'The Pearl'
Family: *Amaryllidaceae*
Height: 60 cm (24 in)

'The Pearl' is a double-flowered variety that can be grown outdoors only in very mild climates. Its bulbs are planted in full sun, 3–5 cm (1–2 in) deep. *Polianthes* prefer a fertile well-drained, humus-rich soil and should be watered regularly. In colder climates, they can also be grown indoors in containers, and brought outdoors only during the summer months.

Ranunculus

Although there are other genera of flowering bulbs in the family Ranunculaceae *(like* Eranthis*), the species in the genus* Ranunculus *are generally not bulbous.* Ranunculus asiaticus, *however, is an exception, because it has tuberous roots.*

Ranunculus asiaticus

Family: *Ranunculaceae*
Height: 40 cm (16 in)

The tuberous roots of *Ranunculus asiaticus* are planted in the spring, 5 cm (2 in) deep and 7–8 cm (2½–3 in) apart, in a sunny location and fertile, well-drained soil. Its stems are 30–60 cm (12–24 in) long and support one double flower. Some varieties, such as 'Peonia,' have flowers that are so full, they are almost beyond double. Ranunculuses bloom throughout the summer in a vivid array of red, pink, yellow, orange and white.

Ranunculus

Sandersonia
CHINESE LANTERN LILY

Sandersonia aurantiaca
Family: *Colchicaceae*
Height: 70 cm (28 in)

Sandersonia aurantiaca is a vine that sometimes grows to almost 1 m (3¼ ft) in height. From July through September, it produces decidedly lantern-shaped, golden yellow, pendant flowers that grow from the leaf axil. Its cylindrical tubers are planted 10–15 cm (4–6 in) deep and 15 cm (6 in) apart.

Chinese lantern lilies will thrive in a sunny location, in well-drained soil that has been amended with sand, and is rich in organic matter. They propagate naturally through the division of their tubers.

234

The genus Sandersonia, belonging to the family Colchicaceae, is comprised of a single species: Sandersonia aurantiaca, also called the Chinese lantern lily due to the unique, lanternlike shape of its flowers.

Sandersonias are native to the rocky and wooded areas of South Africa and can be planted outdoors only in very mild climates. In colder climates, they can be grown indoors or in a greenhouse.

Sandersonia

Scadoxus

Scadoxus multiflorus

Family: *Amaryllidaceae*
Height: 40 cm (16 in)

This species has bright green foliage, with some leaves clustering together while others droop to the ground. Although there are other varieties, like 'Katherinae,' that are 1 m (3¼ ft) tall, *Scadoxus multiflorus* generally does not grow to more than 30–45 cm (12–18 in) in height. Its relatively thick, stalklike stems support almost perfectly spherical umbels that are 10–15 cm (4–6 in) in diameter, and comprised of at least one hundred small, red, star-shaped flowers with thin, spiky petals and elongated stamens that make the umbel look like a levitating ball.

S. multiflorus blooms throughout the summer and prefers partial shade and well-drained soil high in organic matter. Water regularly, but not excessively, throughout the entire vegetative period. Plants can be propagated by separating their bulbils before replanting the bulbs in the spring.

The Scadoxus *genus, belonging to the* Amaryllidaceae *family, includes species that are sometimes also placed in the* Haemanthus *genus.* Scadoxus *are native to the African savannas, but have long since been exported around the world. In most of North America and Europe, they must be grown indoors or in containers that can be brought outdoors during the warm spring and summer months. In particularly mild climates, they can also be overwintered outdoors. In either case, their large bulbs must be planted 10 cm (4 in) deep and 20 cm (8 in) apart.*

Schizostylis
KAFFIR LILY

Schizostylis coccinea
Family: *Iridaceae*
Height: 50 cm (20 in)

Schizostylis coccinea has long, pale green leaves and racemes composed of pink or red star-shaped flowers, depending on the variety. Each raceme is 4–5 cm (1½–2 in) wide.

Schizostylis is a rather delicate plant that sometimes grows to a height of 80–90 cm (31–35 in). It will only grow well in sheltered, sunny locations and cannot tolerate winter frost. Its rhizomes are planted in the spring, in fresh, fertile soil, 7–8 cm (2½–3 in) deep and 10–30 cm (4–12 in) apart. Every April and May, the soil should be covered with a layer of peat and a mulch of leaves to keep the moisture from evaporating.

Because *S. coccinea* does not bloom at the same time as most plants, it is a highly valued cut flower and, with proper care, it grows extremely well in pots.

Propagate every two to three years during the spring by extracting its rhizomes from the soil and dividing them, making sure that each piece has at least three or four buds. *S. coccinea* can be left in the ground year-round, but must be protected by an abundant mulch of ferns and straw.

236

Also included in this section are summer–fall blooming species like the Schizostylis coccinea—a flowering bulb belonging to the family Iridaceae that, in warmer climates, blooms from the last few weeks of summer through November. Kaffir lilies are native to South Africa where, because of the inversion of seasons in the Northern and Southern Hemispheres, they can be found blooming from January to March along the banks of streams in the Drakensberg Mountains.

Schizostylis

Sparaxis

Sparaxis can be overwintered outdoors only where the winters are free of frost. Its corms are planted 7–8 cm (2½–3 in) deep and 10 cm (4 in) apart in fertile, well-drained soil.

Sparaxis tricolor
Family: *Iridaceae*
Height: 25 cm (10 in)

Sparaxis tricolor is of modest size and called the harlequin flower because of its multi-colored flowers. Its blooms have pale pink, orange or magenta petals, each with vivid yellow markings at their centers, made more evident by their irregular black borders. Most corms that are available have been "prepared" for summer blooming. When its leaves have completely withered, its bulbs should be removed from the soil and stored in a dry location until the following planting season. Propagation occurs by the separation of the cormels that form around the larger corms.

Sprekelia
AZTEC LILY

Given their Mexican and Guatemalan origins, Sprekelia are sensitive to cold weather and can be overwintered outdoors only in similarly mild climates.

Sprekelia formosissima
Family: *Amaryllidaceae*
Height: 30 cm (12 in)

The *Sprekelia formosissima*, or Aztec lily, is a plant of modest size, often less than 30 cm (12 in) tall. Although it is not a very cold-hardy species, its small size makes it easy to grow in window boxes or in small pots, and it can therefore be enjoyed in almost any climate. Its large bulbs are planted approximately 8 cm (3 in) deep and 10 cm (4 in) apart.

This species has long, thin leaves and in mid-summer produces a single velvety red flower with bright, contrasting yellow anthers. Its flowers are funnel-shaped and have six tepals, of which the upper three are elegantly slender and outward curving.

Tigridia
TIGER FLOWER

Tiger flowers are native to the prairies of the Mexican plateau and can be over-wintered outdoors only in similarly mild climates. In colder climates they can be grown in containers.

Tigridia pavonia
Family: *Iridaceae*
Height: 40 cm (16 in)

Tigridia pavonia (tiger peacock), named for its unusual flowers, is commonly called both "tiger flower" and "peacock flower." Its highly speckled throat can be orange, red or purple on a white background and is the same color as its outer petals, which are uniform in color.

Tiger flowers can only survive outdoors in very mild climates, but grow well indoors or in a warm greenhouse. They bloom from July through September.

Tritonia

The genus Tritonia, *native to South Africa, includes both summer and winter blooming species. The summer bloomers are slightly hardier and can be grown outdoors in all but the coldest climates.*

Tritonia crocata
Family: *Iridaceae*
Height: 30 cm (12 in)

This species has long, thin, spearlike leaves and spikes of five to 10 funnel-shaped flowers, 2½–4 cm (1–1½ in) in diameter. The classic variety has orange flowers, but white, pink and yellow varieties also exist.

Tritonia crocata bloom from June to August. Its corms are planted in September–October in a cold greenhouse or outdoors in the spring, 5 cm (2 in) deep and 7–8 cm (2½–3 in) apart, in a warm and sunny location. It can be propagated by dividing its corms, which should be extracted from the soil at the end of the growing season and stored in a dry location until the following spring.

Tulbaghia

Tulbaghia, *belonging to the family* Amaryllidaceae, *are native to southern Africa. They have delicate corms and can only be grown outdoors in similarly mild climates, but they can also be grown indoors. The most common species is* Tulbaghia violacea, *sometimes also called* T. fragrans *or* T. pulchella.

Tulbaghia violacea
Family: *Amaryllidaceae*
Height: 45 cm (18 in)

In the garden, its corms are planted 7–8 cm (2½–3 in) deep and 10 cm (4 in) apart in light, sandy, well-drained soil, but it can also be grown in containers. *Tulbaghia violacea* produces delicately perfumed, spherical umbels comprised of 15 to 30 small, funnel-shaped flowers. Its lavender- or orange-tinted white blooms appear from August to October.

Zantedeschia
CALLA LILY

Many of the most popular zantedeschias are original botanical species, such as Z. aethiopica, Z. elliottiana and Z. rehmannii. The development of exciting new shades of yellow, pink, red and orange, however, has only caused their popularity to increase. Zantedeschia are named after the Italian botanist Francesco Zantedeschi, but the name calla lily is more commonly used.

Zantedeschia aethiopica
Family: *Araceae*
Height: 80 cm (31 in)

240

The eternally classic *Zantedeschia aethiopica* is probably the most popular botanical species and is actually taller than the *Zantedeschia* hybrids. Its signature white flower, however, is not really a flower, but a modified leaf, or "spathe" in the form of a large funnel-shaped petal wrapped around a long, pistil-like inflorescence or "spadix" of miniscule yellow flowers. Its swordlike basal leaves are 10 cm (4 in) wide and 20 cm (8 in) long and, depending on the species, can be uniformly green or have light green or silver dots or stripes.

Zantedeschia

Zantedeschia albomaculata

Family: *Araceae*
Height: 60 cm (24 in)

This lovely cream-colored species is similar to the slightly taller *Z. aethiopica*. Like most calla lilies, *Z. albomaculata* has large, spherical, rootlike rhizomes that are covered with "eyes." These "eyes" are actually buds that will begin to grow as soon as the right conditions are provided. Healthy rhizomes should be firm to the touch and stored in a dry location until the next planting season. Under normal circumstances *Z. albomaculata* blooms from mid-summer to mid-fall.

242

Zantedeschia ▼ 'Mango'

Family: *Araceae*
Height: 60 cm (24 in)

This calla lily has marvelous orange blooms that look as if they have been shaded with a colored pencil. Like all calla lilies, 'Mango' loves water and can even tolerate the wet soil found at the edge of a body of a pond or stream, as

Zantedeschia ▲ 'Black Eyed Beauty'

Family: *Araceae*
Height: 60 cm (24 in)

The color of this hybrid falls somewhere in between the white or cream-colored callas (e.g., *Z. aethiopica* and *Z. albomaculata*) and the bright orange or yellow callas (e.g., *Z. elliottiana*).

Its rhizomes are planted 10 cm (4 in) deep, in mild regions,

and can be left in the ground year-round. If rhizomes are to remain in the soil year-round, they should be planted 15 cm (6 in) deep for better insulation from the cold. As far as the planting distance between each rhizome is concerned, the more colorful varieties should be planted 25–30 cm (10–12 in) apart, while the white varieties should be planted 30–40 cm (12–16 in) apart.

long as its roots are not constantly covered with water. If growing in a container, place in a location that is exposed to sun for half the day; this will cause the blooms to last longer. The containers can be placed next to other plants with similar growing requirements.

Zantedeschia ▲ elliottiana
Family: *Araceae*
Height: 60 cm (24 in)

Zantedeschia elliottiana is the yellow-flowered botanical species from which many of the colored hybrids have been derived.

Until the new growth is visible above the soil, irrigation should be kept to a minimum; frequent watering can cause the newly planted rhizomes to rot. The colorful callas need more fertilizer than the white varieties and should be fed once a week from March to September with liquid fertilizer. In regions subject to winter frost, at the end of the growing season, rhizomes must be removed from the soil, dried and stored in wood chips.

Zantedeschia 'Pink Persuasion'

Family: *Araceae*
Height: 50 cm (20 in)

This cultivar's spathe (the modified, flowerlike leaf surrounding the numerous tiny flowers located in the spadix) is very similar in color to 'Mango.'

Calla lilies can be forced to bloom out of season by planting their rhizomes indoors in early spring, in 5 cm (2 in) of soil and watering them twice a week to stimulate the rapid growth of the roots and the first leaves. They can be moved to the garden or to a larger, more beautiful container between May and June.

Zantedeschia 'Suzy'

Family: *Araceae*
Height: 50 cm (20 in)

'Suzy' or 'Little Suzy' is a hybrid that is much admired for its exquisite white and pink flowers. It is easier to grow in containers than the white varieties because, like the other colored callas, it is not as tall. 'Suzy' is also much sought after for its cut flowers and is considered to be among the most elegant and sophisticated calla lilies. Even its leaves (its true leaves, not the spathe) can be used for decorative purposes.

GLOSSARY

Achene A dry indehiscent fruit, containing only one seed, in which the seed coat does not adhere to the seed itself.

Amending the soil Correction of the soil's physical character-istics by adding specific substances, such as sand, manure or peat.

Annual A plant that completes its life cycle within the span of one year.

Anther The tip of the stamen, containing the pollen.

Apex The terminal section of a branch, root or leaf.

Axil The upper angle formed by a leaf or branch and the stem or the trunk.

Bacterium A unicellular microorganism lacking a nucleus and chlorophyll.

Berry A simple fleshy fruit, with seeds immersed in the pulpy mass.

Biennial A plant that com-pletes its life cycle in two growing seasons. During the first year the plant grows foliage and during the second it forms flowers and fruits.

Bone meal Ground bone, raw or steamed, that is used as a fertilizer to add phosphoric acid to the soil.

Border A strip of soil at the edge of a flower bed or run-ning alongside a path in which flowers or other vegetation has been planted.

Bract A modified leaf usually reduced in size.

Bud Small mass of vegetative tissue from which new organs or new plants form.

Bulb The underground organ of some flowering plants, composed of a short, modified stem covered with thick, fleshy leaves (bulb scales) that pro-tect the stem and store food and water.

Bulbil A small bulb that grows spontaneously from another bulb. Also called bulblet.

Caducous Describing the parts of a plant (usually the leaves) that are easily detached or shed at an early stage, usually after one growth season.

Calcareous (soil) Soil contain-ing large quantities of calcium carbonate or lime; chalky.

Calyx The outer protective wrapping of the flower in bud, formed by one or more sepals.

Campanulate Bell-shaped.

Capitulum An inflorescence made up of numerous sessile flowers inserted, one next to the other, on a flat common base and enveloped by bracts simulating a calyx; typical of the Compositae family.

Cell The structural unit of a living organism, consisting of cytoplasm and one or more nuclei enclosed in a membrane.

Cellulose Complex carbohy-drate and primary component in the cell wall of most plants.

Chlorophyll The green pig-ment found in plant cells, needed for photosynthesis.

Chlorosis Yellowing of the leaves caused by the destruction or reduced production of chlorophyll.

Cirrus Tendril-like leaf or branch that plants without stems use to climb by wrapping them around any nearby structure.

Classification In biology, the systematic categorization of organisms into a coherent scheme (e.g., order, genus, family and species).

Clay Any soil particle less than .002 mm (0.00008 in) in diameter.

Clay soil Soil containing a high percentage of clay; it is dense and difficult to work and capable of retaining large amounts of water.

Cold frame Small structure with a glass top, used outdoors to protect plants from the cold, creating an extended growing season.

Compound leaf A leaf whose lamina is divided into many tiny little leaves.

Corm The underground organ of some plants, primarily comprised of stem tissue, and used to store food and water.

Cormel A smaller, secondary corm produced spontaneously by another corm; a bulbil.

Corolla The petals of a flower, located inside the calyx and immediately surrounding the stamens and pistil. Usually the most ornate part of the flower.

Corona A crownlike outgrowth from the inner side of the corolla or perigonium in some flowers, typical to daffodils.

Corymb A flat-topped inflorescence in which flowers, growing at different points on the same axis, grow to be the same height due to their different length peduncles.

Cultivar Cultivated variety of plant.

Cutting Type of agamic propagation that consists in the cutting of a leaf, branch or stem from another plant, and from which roots will soon begin to grow when placed in the soil, eventually forming a new plant.

Deciduous A plant that sheds its leaves annually before entering into its dormant phase.

Dehiscence Opening of an anther, fruit or other structure to release reproductive material, such as pollen or seeds.

Dentate With sharp toothlike edges; serrated.

Diclinous Flowers with only male or only female reproductive organs. Some flowers in the species are male and some are female.

Dormancy Period of the year during which plants are not actively growing.

Drainage The process by which excess water is prevented from accumulating in the soil.

Dwarf (plant) Plant of smaller dimensions, often creeping.

Epiphyte A plant growing on or from another plant, but without being parasitic.

Evergreen Plant that does not lose its leaves at the beginning of the cold season, but stays green year-round.

Family The classification between order and genus. Family names are derived from the name of its primary genus with the suffix "-aceae" for plants.

Female flower A flower with no stamens.

Fertilization The fusion of male and female gametes resulting in the creation of a zygote which becomes the seed.

Fertilizer Product of organic or mineral origin added to the soil to increase its fertility.

Filament Peduncle of the stamen that supports the anther.

Flower Reproductive unit of angiosperms. A complete flower has a perianth (made up of the calyx and corolla), an androecium (the stamens) and a gynoecium (the pistil).

Forcing Series of techniques (usually artificial heat and controlled daylight) used to cause plants to germinate, bloom and produce seeds at a season earlier than their natural one.

Fruit The mature and transformed ovary of an angiosperm containing seeds.

Fungicide A substance used to destroy fungi and bacteria.

Fungus Vegetable organism lacking chlorophyll that can live as a parasite of other organisms or as a saprophyte.

Gall Voluminous malformation caused by insect bites that develops on plants.

Genus A classification of organisms having common characteristics distinct from those of other genera, located between the classifications of family and species.

Germination Initial growth process in seeds, buds or other structures.

Glabrous Hairless, smooth.

Glaucous Blue-green, blue-gray, gray or pale yellow-green color.

Growth season Period during the year during which the plant is actively growing and reproducing.

Half-hardy Any plant able to live outdoors year-round, but in colder climates requires a winter mulch to keep underground organs from freezing.

Hardy Any plant able to tolerate cold winters without protection.

Herbaceous Of or like herbs; not woody.

Honeydew Sticky and sugary liquid secreted by aphids and made up of partially transformed sap.

Humus Partially decomposed organic matter present in the soil.

Hybrid The offspring of two different species or varieties.

Hybridization Crossbreeding of two different species or varieties.

Inflorescence Cluster of flowers along the same axis.

Insecticide Natural or chemical product used to kill or repel insects.

Internode The part of the stem between any two consecutive nodes.

Lacinia Narrow, irregular lobes of petals or leaves.

Lamina The extended and flat part of the leaf.

Lanceolate Long and thin leaf tapering to a point like a lance; lance-shaped.

Leaf One of the most important organs of a plant; it performs various functions, the most important of which is photosynthesis.

Leaf mold A compost of decayed leaves. It can be used, alone or mixed with other substances, as a soil for growing plants.

Limestone A sedimentary rock composed primarily of calcium carbonate, commonly ground and used as fertilizer. Limestone makes soil more alkaline and easier to work.

Linear Long and very narrow with parallel sides, such as a linear leaf.

Loam The textural class named for soil containing 7 percent to

22 percent clay, 28 percent to 50 percent silt and less than 52 percent sand. Also a general term referring to a mellow soil rich in organic matter.

Male flower A flower lacking a pistil.

Manure An organic fertilizer derived from fermented animal dung.

Metabolism The sum of all chemical processes that occur in a cell or in a living organism.

Mulch A mixture of straw, peat, manure, etc., spread on the ground to reduce moisture loss, prevent weed growth or keep the ground from freezing.

Node The part of the stem from which one or more leaves grow.

Order The classification above a class and below a family.

Organ Structure composed of differentiated tissues, such as the stem, leaves, flowers, etc.

Ovary Located at the bottom of the pistil and containing the ovules. The ovary becomes the fruit.

Panicle An inflorescence comprised of a principal axis from which secondary axes branch out in clusters.

Parasite Any organism that lives off and causes damage to another organism.

Peat Partially decomposed organic matter found in particularly humid and cold locations called peat bogs.

Peduncle The stem of a flower or inflorescence.

Perigonium The tepals of a flower.

Petal Usually brightly colored part of a flower's corolla.

Pistil The female reproductive organ found in angiosperms, consisting of the ovary, the style and the stigma.

Pollen Fine grains emitted from the pollen sacs located on the anthers and containing the male gametes.

Pollination The process by which pollen is transferred from the anthers to the stigma.

Pseudobulb A fleshy enlargement resembling a bulb at the base of the stem.

Raceme An inflorescence with an elongated primary axis along which flowers on equal length peduncles grow.

Rhizome An underground, horizontally growing, modified root.

Root The underground part of the plant that absorbs water and minerals from the soil, transfers them to the other parts of the plant and also acts as an anchor.

Sand soil particle 0.02–2 mm (0.0008–0.08 in) in diameter.

Sap A watery substance circulating in plants that contains minerals, sugars and other organic substances.

Scales The thick, fleshy, concentric layers of modified leaves of bulbs that store food and protect the short stem.

Scape The stem of any herbaceous plant with a flower or inflorescence at one end.

Seed The organ formed by the maturation of the ovule after fertilization and comprised of an embryo, food storage and a seed coat.

Sepal A modified leaf of the calyx.

Sessile A leaf without a petiole, or a flower or fruit without a peduncle.

Simple leaf An undivided leaf.

Soil The top layer of the earth's crust, modified by living organisms and climate.

Solum The layer of soil in which the roots of plants grow.

Spadix An inflorescence typical to the Araceae family wrapped in a spathe.

Spathe The modified and often colorful leaf that wraps around the inflorescence of members of the Araceae family.

Species A classification that groups together individuals able to reproduce. Species names are made up of two parts and written in a different typeface (e.g., *Zantedeschia aethiopica*).

Sphagnum moss A particular type of moss that grows in cold, damp environments, like peat bogs.

Spike An inflorescence with a primary axis along which sessile flowers grow.

Spur The rear portion of the corolla that is cylindrical, straight or curved, and of varying dimensions.

Stamen The pollen-producing male reproductive organ of a flower made up of the filament and the anthers.

Stem The arial axis of a vascular plant. The stem has many functions: it supports the leaves and flowers, it stores and conducts nutrients from one part of the plant to the other and in some cases it also performs photosynthesis. Underground parts of the plant with analogous anatomical structures, such as tubers, rhizomes, etc., are also considered stems.

Stigma The top portion of the pistil where the pollen is deposited.

Stolon A slender stem that occasionally forms roots.

Style The filamentous, tubelike portion of the pistil that connects the ovary to the stigma.

Subspecies Subdivision of a species.

Tegument The protective layer around the ovule that becomes the seed coat.

Tepal The petals of a flower when the calyx and corolla are not clearly differentiated, as in tulips.

Tomentum A covering of downy hair usually found on leaves and young stems.

Topsoil The fertile top layer of soil usually found in woods and meadows, rich in organic matter.

Tuber An underground, modified and enlarged stem that stores nutrients.

Tubercle A tuberous root bearing adventitious buds and which functions like a tuber.

Tuberous root A modified root that stores food rather than absorbing nutrients from the soil.

Tunic The thin, papery covering that surrounds some bulbs.

Umbel An inflorescence in which the single peduncles are all attached at the same point on the scape.

Variegated Having two or more colors.

Variety Subdivision of a species that groups individuals with certain like characteristics. Varieties can be artificial or naturally occurring.

Vegetative propagation Asexual reproduction of a plant by means of bulbils, leaf cuttings, stem cuttings, layering or root division.

Venation The web of veins in a leaf.

Vermiculite A granular substance used for its unique ability to retain water to grow plants in containers.

Voluble A plant that is unable to sustain its own weight and must be held up with a support stake.

Arrigoni, O. *Elementi di biologia vegetale* (Fundamentals of Plant Biology). Milan: Casa Editrice Ambrosiana, 1980.

Bonciarelli, F. *Agronomia* (Agronomy). Bologna: Edagricole, 1980.

Cocker, H.R., and G. Oelker. *Le Bulbose* (Bulbs). Bologna: Edagricole, 1979.

Crockett, James U. *Bulbs: The Time-Life Encyclopedia of Gardening*. New York: Henry Holt and Co., 1987.

Dykes, William Rickatson. *The Genus Iris*. New York: Dover Publications, 1974.

Grey-Wilson, C., and Brian Mathew. *Bulbs*. London: Collins, 1981.

Hessayon, D.G. *The Bulb Expert*. London: Expert Books, 1995.

Jekyll, Gertrude. *Lilies for English Gardens*. Antique Collectors' Club, 1982.

Mathew, D., and P. Swindells. *The Gardener's Guide to Bulbs*. Mitchell Beazley Limited, 1994.

Moggi, Guido, and Luciano Giugnolini. *Simon & Schuster's Guide to Garden Flowers*. New York: Simon & Schuster, 1983.

Papworth, David. *Illustrated Guide to Bulbs*. Toronto: Salamander Press, 1986.

Pignatti, S. *Flora d'Italia* (Flora of Italy). Bologna: Edagricole, 1982.

Porro, E. *I Gladioli* (Gladioli). Milan: De Vecchi Editore, 1975.

Raven, Peter H., Ray F. Evert and Susan Eichhorn. *The Biology of Plants*. New York: W.H. Freeman and Co., 1998.

Rix, Martyn, and Roger Phillips. *The Random House Book of Bulbs*. New York: Random House, 1989.

Royal Horticultural Society. *Bulbs*. London: Dorling Kindersley Limited, 1997.

Schauenberg, P. *Les Plantes Bulbeuses* (Bulbous plants). Neuchâtel: Delachaux et Niestlé, 1964.

Schönfelder, I., and P. Schönfelder. *Impariamo a Conoscere la Flora Mediterrananea* (Learning to Recognize Mediterranean Flora). Novara: Istituto Geografico De Agostini, 1986.

Servadei, A, S. Zangheri and L. Masutti. *Entomologia Generale e Applicata* (General and Applied Entomology). Padua: CEDAM, 1972.

Springer, G. *How to Grow a Miracle*. Netherlands: John Boswell Associates Book, 1968.

Il grande libro dei fiori e delle piante (The Big Book of Flowers and Plants). Milan: Selezione dal Reader's Digest, 1978.

Wright, M. *Le Più Belle* (The Most Beautiful). Milan: Centro Botanico, 1987.